ADAM RUINS
EVERYTHING

FOREWORD BY ADAM CONOVER

A POST HILL PRESS BOOK
ISBN: 978-1-68261-508-9

Adam Ruins Everything
© 2018 truTV
All Rights Reserved

Post Hill Press
New York • Nashville
posthillpress.com

Published in the United States of America

TABLE OF CONTENTS

FOREWORD

Adam Ruins Everything is a show about the awful truth behind everything you take for granted. So, when I was asked to write the foreword to the *Adam Ruins Everything* Episode Guide, I knew that holding back wasn't an option: It's my responsibility—nay, my sworn duty—to reveal the hidden truth about the very book you hold in your hands. So, without further ado, I present the *Adam Ruins Everything* Episode Guide.

ACT ONE: YOU'LL NEVER READ THIS BOOK

As a society, we much prefer the fun and exciting process of buying books—the thrill of clicking "Checkout" on Amazon! The charming snobbery of your local bookstore! The intoxicating smell of fresh glue and ink, to the boring and time-consuming chore of, you know, actually reading them. One survey found that half the books in the average home have never been read. *Source: telegraph. co.uk/culture/books/10679079/Half-of-books-in-homes-are-unread.html.*

Face facts: Those expensive, heavy tomes lining our shelves are pretty much just for decoration.

ACT TWO: YOU SHOULDN'T READ THIS BOOK

Honestly, it's no wonder so few of us read the books we buy—we simply don't have enough time. Even if you were to read a book a week starting from the moment you left the birth canal, you'd only have time to get through a few thousand before you died. *Source: telegraph.co.uk/culture/books/10679079/Half-of-books-in-homes-are-unread.html.*

The number of informative, spectacular, mind-expanding books you will never have time to read is truly staggering. So let's be perfectly frank: You need to prioritize. Even if you *were* going to read this book, would it be worth it when you could be consuming a classic work like *Moby-Dick,* or challenging yourself with one of Ta-Nehisi Coates's searing critiques instead? I don't think so.

ACT THREE: THIS BOOK CONTAINS NO NEW CONTENT ANYWAY

When we buy a book, our expectation is that it contains new information about the topic at hand. Ground-breaking research! Never-before-told stories! Salacious behind-the-scenes dirt! Sorry: You won't find those things here. This is the *Adam Ruins Everything* Episode Guide. That means it's exclusively composed of *summaries* of episodes of television you've already seen. I mean seriously, we're talking beat-for-beat transcriptions of our scripts, laid out in book format. The fact is that if you're a fan of *Adam Ruins Everything* (and if you're not, why would you buy this book?), then you are already intimately familiar with every fact, story, and citation lying between these two covers. The only exception: the foreword you're reading right now. Hope you're getting your money's worth!

Now, if you're anything like the typical *Adam Ruins Everything* character, you're seeing red right now: "You're telling me this book is nothing but a cynical cash grab by a major media corporation?

And not only will I never read it, even if I did it would be a waste of time?" But if you're anything like the typical *Adam Ruins Everything* viewer, you're smart enough to know what the answer is: "Yes, all of that is true. But that doesn't mean this book is useless! In fact, there are *plenty* of reasons it's still worth owning! And I'll tell you all about it right after this...paragraph."

ACT FOUR: THE POSITIVE TAKEAWAY

If we do not read the books we buy, then why do we buy them to begin with? Well, for a whole host of reasons that I'll discuss below.

THEY SERVE AS PHYSICAL TOKENS OF OUR INTERESTS

Though the digital age of media has its conveniences, it's also ephemeral as all heck. Our favorite shows are on Netflix, our favorite music is on Spotify—heck, even comic book fans are giving up the cardboard backing and the plastic bags in favor of keeping up with their favorite superheroes on digital apps. We've all embraced this new, download-on-demand world with gusto. But still, we all feel something missing, don't we? Our favorite things seem to lack weight and solidity, instead floating away like mist on the breeze. Sometimes we love a particular piece of media so much that we just want it *in our goddamn house.*[1]

It's this desire, I think, that's behind the resurgence of vinyl. Despite the fact that vinyl doesn't actually sound better than high-resolution digital audio files, many music fans, myself included, prefer to listen to music on vinyl. *Source: vox.com/2014/4/19/5626058/vinyls-great-but-its-not-better-than-cds*

Why? Well, one reason is that if you love a piece of media, owning it in physical form deepens your relationship with that media. Being able to literally touch the music and display it in my home actually makes me like it more.

---

1. *Or apartment!* There's nothing wrong with renting; see Season 1 Episode 19, "Adam Ruins Housing," for more information.

Now, this book may not be as beautiful as a first pressing of *Sgt. Pepper's Lonely Hearts Club Band*, but the principle may still apply. If you're an *Adam Ruins Everything* fan, and feel like you'll deepen your appreciation of the show by holding the first season of the show in your hot little hands, well, by God, that feeling is real and deserves to be cherished.

IT SUPPORTS THE ART WE LOVE

truTV put out this book for a simple reason: Television is dying. By the end of 2017, twenty-two million U.S. adults will have cancelled their pay TV subscriptions. *Source: variety.com/2017/biz/news/cord-cutting-2017-estimates-cancel-cable-satellite-tv-1202556594/*

And while the rise of streaming platforms and internet video has brought millions of new viewers to shows like ours (I can't count the number of fans who tell me "I love you on YouTube!"), the ad dollars haven't followed. I don't know whether our show is profitable or not, but I do know that when I ask the network executives that question, their smiles get tighter than a ventriloquist dummy with lockjaw.

Thus, this book. By selling copies of a physical object to fans of the show, the network is able to recoup some of the cost of making the show, and maybe even turn up a profit on their balance sheet. Fans (especially the fans who download our show on BitTorrent, bless them) often ask me, "How can I support your show?" Let me tell you plainly: Buying this book supports our show effectively and directly, because the more money the network can make from it, the more episodes they'll be incentivized to produce.

THEY COMMUNICATE OUR VALUES BACK TO OURSELVES

Forget why we buy books: Why do we arrange them on our shelves? Why do we display them, spines out to the world, as though they were beloved relics? Simple: Because we feel that the books we own say something about us. And while it's certainly tempting to view this behavior cynically, as an example of vain humans trying to show off to our friends, I think there's something subtler going on.

The English author Arnold Bennett wrote in his essay "The Philosophy of Book Buying":

> All impassioned bookmen, except a few who devote their whole lives to reading, have rows of books on their shelves which they have never read, and which they never will read. I know that I have hundreds such. My eye rests on the works of Berkeley in three volumes, with a preface by the Right Honorable Arthur James Balfour. I cannot conceive the circumstances under which I shall ever read Berkeley; but I do not regret having bought him in a good edition, and I would buy him again if I had him not; for when I look at him some of his virtue passes into me; I am the better for him. A certain aroma of philosophy informs my soul, and I am less crude than I should otherwise be. This is not fancy, but fact. *Source: The Philosophy of Book Buying.*

In other words, we buy books to remind ourselves of our values—not just those we possess, but those we hope to cultivate and coax into being.

Our intention in creating *Adam Ruins Everything* was to produce a show that stands for skepticism, reason, empathy, and above all, boundless curiosity. If having this book on your shelf will help you remember those values and live them out in your life, then I think that might be worth the sticker price.

If it won't, then please: Put this book back on the bookstore shelf (or close the "Look Inside" preview on your Amazon tab—I know what decade this is), and walk away. The last thing I would want you to do is spend money on a product that gives you no value; that would make this book little more than a scam itself. The choice, in the end, is yours.

Either way: Thanks for watching our weird little show, and thanks for always seeking to know more about the world around you.

Stay curious,

Adam Conover

EPISODE ONE

ADAM RUINS

GIVING

DIRECTOR: PAUL BRIGANTI

ORIGINAL AIR DATE: SEPTEMBER 29, 2015

Giving is generally considered to be a good thing. We're helping our fellow human beings and all that. Turns out, though, that giving kind of sucks—at least when it comes to the way most people do it.

PUTTING A RING ON IT

Adam's first "giving" target is the practice of buying an engagement ring. Most folks think of it as some kind of timeless ritual. It ain't. In actuality, the whole goofy thing was created by the De Beers Diamond Corporation less than a century ago.

In 1938, De Beers launched a massive ad campaign implying that the only way for a real man to show his love was with a hunk of crystallized carbon—and we bought it. *Source: Epstein, Edward Jay. "Have You Ever Tried to Sell a Diamond?" The Atlantic. Atlantic Media Company, 01 Feb. 1982.*

You might be thinking: "But diamonds are super rare and have value and all that crap, right?" Nope. De Beers's chairman, Nicky Oppenheimer, was once quoted as saying, "Diamonds are intrinsically worthless." *Source: Feb. 13, 1999, The Independent.*

A word from
EDWARD JAY EPSTEIN,
Author of *The Rise and Fall of Diamonds: The Shattering of a Brilliant Illusion*:

"When I was writing my book, I took a diamond that someone had paid 6,000 dollars for the day before, and I took it from one diamond store to another diamond store in New York. And you know what I was offered? Less than 1,000 dollars.

"That diamond had lost five-sixth of its value overnight."

The thing is, diamonds aren't rare at all. In fact, they're quite common. The only reason diamonds are even expensive is that De Beers had a global monopoly on diamond mining, and they artificially restricted the supply to jack the prices up. But in reality, those buttholes have a poop ton of them.

That's why De Beers wants us to think a diamond is forever. As long as we never try to sell them, we'll never figure out how badly we got screwed—and continue to get screwed.

WAITING FOR THE OTHER SHOE TO DROP

We all know TOMS Shoes. Their "buy one, give one" business model has made them massively successful.

Well, there is no Tom.

The real owner of TOMS is a guy named Blake Mycoskie. Which you would know if you checked Blake's bio on the TOMS corporate website. And as noble as Blake's intentions may be, the "buy one, give one" model is incredibly misguided.

Before Blake founded TOMS, he was a reality star who appeared on CBS's *The Amazing Race* and *FOX's Sexiest Bachelor in America* pageant. Source: Costello, Amy. "TOMS Shoes: A Closer Look." Audio blog post. Tiny Spark. Tiny Spark, n.d.

AS NOT SEEN ON TV ✂

This pilot episode contains the show's first viral hit—the segment on engagement rings that Adam created and produced with College Humor. The video was so popular that it got the team thinking, "Hmm...could this be a TV show?"

Those TOMS giveaways have serious ramifications, too. One study showed that free clothing donations to Africa reduced employment in their garment industry by half. Source: Frazer, Garth. "Used-Clothing Donations and Apparel Production in Africa." The Economic Journal 118.532 (2008): 1764-784.

Here's the kicker: The shoes TOMS gives away costs them only four dollars to make. So if they cost sixty dollars, and you get four-dollar shoes—then a kid in Africa gets four-dollar shoes—that means the rest goes to Blake Mycoskie. *Source: McDonald, Patrick Range. "Is Blake Mycoskie of Toms an Evangelical?" LA Weekly (Los Angeles) 28 July 2011: n. pag.*

In 2016, Blake sold his stake in TOMS through a deal valued at 600 million dollars. *Source: Stock, Kyle. "Bain Capital Buys Toms, Will Still Give Away Shoes." Bloomberg Business. Bloomberg, 21 Aug. 2014.*

DID YOU KNOW:

"AN APPLE A DAY KEEPS THE DOCTOR AWAY" IS JUST AN AD SLOGAN CREATED BY THE APPLE INDUSTRY.

IN FACT, UNTIL THE LATE NINETEENTH CENTURY, APPLES WERE EXCLUSIVELY USED TO MAKE HARD CIDER.

Source: Pollan, Michael. The Botany of Desire: A Plant's Eye View of the World. New York: Random House, 2001.

TMS "TEDDY" RUGE,

Founder of Raintree Farms, LTD. In Uganda, they supply high-quality products that contain a nutrient-dense plant called moringa.

Do you have shoes in Uganda?

"Teddy" Ruge: "Surprisingly, yes we do have shoes. We also have shoe stores and we also have cobblers."

But what about those TOMS ads, you know, with all the videos of the shoeless children?

"Teddy" Ruge: "That's what we call 'poverty porn.' They find the most extreme situations and make it look like the most common situation on the continent. Shoes is the least of our problems, really guys. We're worried about malaria, we're worried about getting jobs, we're just worried about having electricity in the village, for example."

Well, if those kids don't need free shoes, why do they take them in the first place?

"Teddy" Ruge: "A kid doesn't understand the ramifications of me receiving these free shoes from somebody in America."

Like what kind of ramifications?

"Teddy" Ruge: "Well, what it does is actually put people who are creating shoes right out of business, and takes away the agency of the community to be self-sustaining."

GIVING BLOOD CAN SUCK

Mass blood drives became an American civic tradition during World War II, when huge amounts of blood were needed by the military. Whenever there's a tragedy in the news, we all reflexively rush to have our veins vacuumed.

The problem is, when everyone in the country does this, we end up with a lot more blood than we actually need.

This wouldn't be a problem, except that blood expires after just forty-two days. *Source: Raymond. "Getting Too Much of a Good Thing." The New York Times. The New York Times, 11 Nov. 2001.*

After September 11 prompted patriotic Americans to donate in record numbers, blood banks were forced to trash over 300,000 pints of blood. Those donations were made with the best of intentions, but they didn't help anyone. *Source: Starr, Douglas. "Bad Blood: The 9/11 Blood-Donation Disaster." The New Republic. The New Republic, 29 July 2002.*

Except maybe vampires.

The worst part is, blood banks need donations year-round. And most of the time, only 5 percent of eligible Americans donate. So, if you really want to help after a disaster, wait a few months and donate blood then. And then keep donating—like, all the time.

FOOD DRIVES AREN'T THE SOLUTION TO THE HUNGER CRISIS

The hungry in America don't want your crummy old food any more than you do. You know the first thing the food pantry does with our old cans? They throw half of them out. *Source: United States. UW Extension. Nutrition Education Program. Keep or Toss Survey For Foods Donated To Food Pantries Summary of 2013 Survey Results.*

Then, someone has to pay to haul all of the donations to a warehouse. Someone has to sort and throw out all the expired cans. Plus, canned food is high in sodium, which causes high blood pressure—which can cause heart problems.

Nearly half the food we donate doesn't meet basic nutritional standards. *Source: Yglesias, Matthew. "Charities Need Your Money, Not Your Random Old Food." Slate. The Slate Group, 7 Dec. 2011.*

As it turns out, the best thing you can do to help feed the needy is to give food banks money. Just money.

IMPORTANT FACT:

ONE IN SEVEN AMERICANS RELY ON FOOD PANTRIES TO HELP FEED THEIR FAMILIES.

Source: United States. USDA. USDA Economic Research Report. By Alisha Coleman-Jensen, Christian Gregory, and Anita Singh. Vol. 173. Washington DC: USDA, 2014.

GENEVIEVE RIUTORT,

Chief Development Officer at Westside Food Bank, California

Why do food drives suck?

Genevieve Riutort: "Canned food drives don't suck, but they're not the most efficient way to give."

And you run a food bank, so you'd know....

Genevieve Riutort: "Yeah, I do. And at our food bank, we have a lot of canned food drives, but they're a whole lot of work. And sometimes we have to throw away food, and there's some costs involved in that."

But there are benefits, right?

Genevieve Riutort: "Well, yeah, I mean, one of the things that's great is it can help children connect to giving. Maybe they'll go out and shop for their favorite canned food or soup, and knowing that another child is going to get it, really helps to make that connection with giving."

Well, that sounds like a good thing.

Genevieve Riutort: "The truth is, the best way to help a food bank is to donate money. Because we buy food on a wholesale level and we work with farmers, so we can take the dollar that you might spend on a single can of beans and turn it into exponentially more food."

SO WHAT ELSE IS A HORRIBLE WASTE OF TIME?

Coat drives.

Ninety percent of what's collected by coat drives is recycled for scrap. Source: Lee, Mike. "The Truth About Where You're Donated Clothes End Up." ABC News. ABC. New York, NY, 21 Dec. 2006. ABC News.

Free farm animals.

A lot of the people who get free farm animals just sell them. Source: Sun, Joy. "Should You Donate Differently?" TED@NYC. New York. Lecture.

JOKE TIME:

WHAT DO RELIEF GROUPS CALL THE DELUGE OF UNNEEDED SUPPLIES WE SEND TO DISASTER AREAS?

THE SECOND DISASTER.

Source: Islam, Moin, Katherine Dolan, John Heggestuen, Alex Nordenson, and John Vande Vate. "Who Is Responsible for the 'Second Disaster'?" Stanford Social Innovation Review. Stanford Social Innovation Review. Stanford University, 29 July 2013.

CONFIRMED AS NONSENSE: SODA CAN TAB DRIVES

People all over America collect them for charity, which is weird, because they're totally worthless. Source: Mikkelson, Barbara. "Keeping Tabs." Snopes.com: Pull Tab Redemption Rumor. Urban Legends Reference Pages, 24 Mar. 2012.

WHAT CAN YOU DO?

You might not like it, but there's one gift that costs nothing to ship and that everybody needs. The single most empowering gift ever invented: money.

Sophal Ear, Associate Professor of Diplomacy and World Affairs at Occidental College:

"If you really want to help people, if you really want to make a difference, the best way is to give money directly.

"Lots of studies across the board have shown that money allows people to buy the things they need and helps local economies. People do spend money on selfish things, but usually those selfish things make them better off. And it could be things like their business or their children's education or their healthcare."

EPISODE TWO

ADAM RUINS SECURITY

DIRECTOR: PAUL BRIGANTI
ORIGINAL AIR DATE: OCTOBER 6, 2015

As you've always suspected, all that security we surround ourselves with doesn't make us any safer. In this episode, Adam broke down why.

THE TSA ISN'T VERY GOOD AT ITS JOB

There's very little evidence that the TSA has ever stopped a terrorist, let alone one with a bomb. *Source: Lapidos, Juliet. "Does the TSA Ever Catch Terrorists?" Slate. Slate, 18 Nov. 2010. Web.*

They didn't stop the shoe bomber, they didn't stop the underwear bomber, heck, they probably won't stop the crop top bomber.

AS NOT SEEN ON TV ✂

The actress Sasha A. Ali, who played a TSA agent in this episode, nailed her character and cracked up Adam and the team so much that she was brought back to play similar characters in several subsequent episodes. Keep an eye out for her!

SO, WHAT *DID* STOP ALL THOSE BOMBS?

Easy: All the other security measures we added since September 11.

The American airline industry has added reinforced cockpit blast doors, more air marshals, and there's the heightened awareness of passengers like you and me. Heck, intelligence agencies work to stop attacks before they even happen. *Source: Hawley, Kip. "Why Airport Security Is Broken—And How To Fix It." Editorial. Wall Street Journal [New York] 15 Apr. 2012, Saturday Essay ed.: n. pag. Web.*

The TSA is also straight-up bad at screening. When the Department of Homeland Security tested them, the TSA failed to find mock weapons and explosives 95 percent of the time. *Source: Fishel, Justin, Pierre Thomas, Mike Levine, and Jack Date. "EXCLUSIVE: Undercover DHS Tests Find Security Failures at US Airports." Good Morning America. ABC. New York, New York, 1 June 2015. ABC News. Web.*

THE CONCEPT OF "SECURITY THEATER"

Security Theater is a show the agency puts on to make it look like they're doing a lot to protect us—even though they aren't.

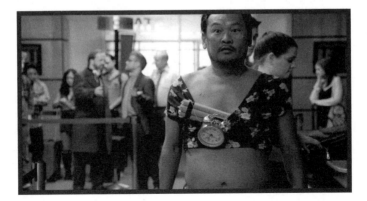

BRUCE SCHNEIER,

Expert on Security Theater:

"As far as screening goes, what we had before September 11 is actually quite adequate. Taking your shoes off and putting your liquids in a separate bag doesn't actually make you safer. It just makes you feel safer.

"First, the illusion of security isn't worth it if you have to give up essential freedoms and privacies to get it.

"Secondly, it's dangerous to present the illusion of security when the system is actually quite vulnerable to terrorist attacks.

"Even if this screening worked, it would only protect us against the last way we were attacked. It does nothing to stop terrorists from finding new ways to hurt us.

"The terrorists can see our security, can figure out how to get around it, so instead of trying to make airports impregnable, we should take the money we're wasting on the TSA and spend it on things that work—intelligence, investigation, and emergency response."

TAMPER-RESISTANT SEALS ARE MORE SECURITY THEATER

In 1982, seven people were killed from cyanide placed inside Tylenol bottles. We don't know who did it, and we don't know why they did it, but let's make the educated guess that it was a crazy person. This left Tylenol with a PR problem. They yanked Tylenol off the shelves, and a few months later, introduced the world to the first tamper resistant seal. *Source: Markel, Howard, Dr. "How the Tylenol Murders of 1982 Changed the Way We Consume Medication." PBS. PBS, 29 Sept. 2014. Web.*

The public was reassured. Tylenol sales completely rebounded, and every other medicine soon did the same. It may make you feel safer, but it doesn't actually protect you from murderers. *Source: Schneier, Bruce. "The Security Mirage." The Security Mirage. Penn State University, University Park. 5 June 2015. TED. Web.*

Think about it, if a real wackadoo really wanted to hurt you, you think a little piece of plastic is gonna stop him?

150 people die every year from what's in over-the-counter pain relief bottles. *Source: Gerth, Jeff, and T. Christian Miller. "Use Only as Directed." ProPublica. ProPublica, 20 Sept. 2013. Web.*

The safety margin between "safe" and "deadly" with Tylenol is way too close for comfort. The company says six pills is a safe daily dosage. *Source: "TYLENOL® Dosage for Adults." Tylenol.com. McNeil Consumer Healthcare Division of McNEIL-PPC, Inc., 2015. Web.*

The FDA says ten pills is a dangerous daily dose. *Source: United States. Food & Drug Administration. ProPublica. By Janet Woodcock. ProPublica, 26 Feb. 2008. Web. 10 Aug. 2015.*

Acetaminophen, the active ingredient in Tylenol, is the number one cause of acute liver failure in America. In one year alone, it's sent as many as 78,000 people to the hospital. *Source: Manthripragada, AD, EH Zhou, DS Budnitz, MC Lovegrove, and ME Willy. "Result Filters." National Center for Biotechnology Information. U.S. National Library of Medicine National Institutes of Health, 20 Aug. 2011. Web.*

Yes, this is all legal.

But a lot of doctors don't think it should be. A 1975 article called "Paracetamol Hepatotoxicity," published by the medical journal *The Lancet*, argued that if the drug were discovered today, it would never be freely available without a prescription.

As for where the FDA is in all of this, the FDA didn't even require them to put a warning label on the bottle until 2009.

DR. SIDNEY WOLFE,
Physician and Co-founder of
Public Citizen's Health Research Group:

"Not only is acetaminophen the leading cause of acute liver failure, but it exceeds all other causes combined. I served on an FDA advisory committee that voted overwhelmingly to lower the maximum non-prescription dose of acetaminophen. But for the past six years, the FDA leadership has effectively ignored our important recommendation. The FDA has essentially failed to protect people from preventable liver toxicity."

CREDIT CARD SIGNATURES? MORE SECURITY THEATER.

There's no handwriting expert at the bank scouring paper trails to approve every signature. They don't sound the alarm when they think they've spotted an aberration in the way you cross your Ts or dot your Is. Nothing happens. *Source: "The Bryant Park Project." Why Do We Still Have To Sign Credit Card Receipts? NPR. New York, New York, 7 July 2008. NPR. Web.*

Then what secures your credit card? Again, nothing.

The credit card system is a pre-internet relic with virtually no built-in security. All a thief needs to purchase something as "you" is the string of numbers on your card. And it's not private information. You give out your credit card number every time you buy something with it.

In the internet age, it is impossible to keep a single sixteen-digit number a secret. Credit card fraud is so pervasive, banks have started just covering the charges so people don't freak out and cancel their cards. *Source: Palmer, Kimberly. "How Credit Card Companies Spot Fraud Before You Do." U.S. News & World Report Money. US. News & World Report L.P., 10 July 2013. Web.*

There is nothing that you can personally do to stop credit card theft.

KEVIN POULSEN,

Journalist, Author of the Book *Kingpin*, and an Expert on Computer Crime:

Kevin Poulsen: "The truth is, there are so many stolen credit card numbers out there that thieves are buying and selling them as commodities. So, here's a website where you can buy credit card numbers for around five dollars a piece. Crooks buy these by the tens, by the hundreds, and this isn't even a dark website—this is a website that anybody could easily search for and find. It's grade school level stuff."

So what can you do?

Kevin Poulsen: "Nothing. It's a systemic problem. Credit card numbers are static and unchanging. Good security is dynamic and it changes every time."

Are there any technological solutions?

Kevin Poulsen: "In Europe, they have something called 'chip and pin' and 'chip and signature.' This is a much more secure way of handling credit card transactions. It's only just now coming to the United States, which means for the next few years, we're still gonna be vulnerable."

He's about
to drop some
knowledge

WHAT CAN YOU DO?

You can relax, for one. You and your family have nothing to worry about. We have weak, imperfect security everywhere in life, and it's totally fine. You know that no one's gonna go through the effort to get into your old shed, so you don't have to stress out about making it perfectly safe. You can take that off of yourself. You have to trust other people to some extent. We're fortunate to live in a pretty safe country, and we make it safer when we build our security systems rationally—based on trust rather than fear. So relax and trust each other. Almost all humans are good people.

to drop some
knowledge

EPISODE THREE

ADAM RUINS

CARS

DIRECTOR: PAUL BRIGANTI

ORIGINAL AIR DATE: OCTOBER 13, 2015

In this episode, Adam revealed the surprising truths behind car dealerships, unearthed the dirty little secrets of car ownership, explained how auto-manufacturers turned "jaywalking" into a crime, and much more.

FUN FACT: CAR DEALERSHIPS ARE PREDATORY BUSINESSES.

And they wield a ton of power.

Dealerships aren't owned by the carmakers, but are separate businesses. *Source: Surowiecki, James. "Dealer's Choice." The New Yorker. Conde Nast, 4 Sept. 2006. Web.*

And since the '30s, dealership associations have pressured every state into passing franchise laws that give them a virtual monopoly over new car sales.

These laws actually make it illegal to sell new cars unless you're a car dealership. And if you want to become a dealer, too bad. It's also illegal to open a new dealership in another dealer's territory. *Source: Lafontaine, Francine, and Fiona Scott Morton. "Markets State Franchise Laws, Dealer Terminations, and the Auto Crisis." Journal of Economic Perspectives 24.3 (2010): 233-50. Yale University. Web.*

The law also makes it nearly impossible for car makers to shut down dealerships—even when they suck. Which means they end up getting passed from father to son, like family dynasties.

20 percent of state sales tax revenue comes from car dealerships, which means dealership owners and their friends pretty much run the show. *Source: Lafontaine, Francine, and Fiona Scott Morton. "Markets State Franchise Laws, Dealer Terminations, and the Auto Crisis." Journal of Economic Perspectives 24.3 (2010): 233-50. Yale University. Web.*

HOW THE AUTOMOBILE TOOK OVER THE AMERICAN STREET

A century ago, the city street was a public place that was open to everyone. *Source: Norton, Peter. "Street Rivals Jaywalking and the Invention of the Motor Age Street." Technology and Culture 48 (2007): 331-59. Vox. Vox Media. Web.*

It was shared by pedestrians, horses, and weird old-timey bicyclists alike. Not to mention streetcars that took people to work. *Source: Stromberg, Joseph. "The Real Story behind the Demise of America's Once-mighty Streetcars." Vox. Vox Media, 07 May 2015. Web.*

But when the car was invented, people started driving them at top speed through the crowded streets, and the results weren't pretty. Naturally, everyone blamed the new invention for the carnage. Public outcry grew. Some cities even discussed passing laws against cars. *Source: Norton, Peter D. Fighting Traffic: The Dawn of the Motor Age in the American City. Cambridge, MA: MIT, 2008. Print.*

In response, the auto industry launched its own campaign. One in which pedestrians who happened to be in the street at the same time as cars were portrayed as deserving of their fate. This is where the term "jaywalking" comes from. To publicize their new insult, the auto-industry actually planted stories in newspapers blaming pedestrians for automobile deaths. *Source: Norton, Peter. "Street Rivals Jaywalking and the Invention of the Motor Age Street." Technology and Culture 48 (2007): 331-59. Vox. Vox Media. Web.*

THE AUTOMOBILE KILLED PUBLIC TRANSPORTATION

Before the car, we had a fast, efficient way to get around cities: the streetcar. At the time, almost every major city had them. But the automobile killed them. *Source: Stromberg, Joseph. "The Real Story behind the Demise of America's Once-mighty Streetcars." Vox. Vox Media, 07 May 2015. Web.*

A single streetcar can carry dozens of pedestrians. But, put each of those passengers in their own car, and they take up one hundred square feet each. And that means one thing: traffic. *Source: Werbach, Adam. "The American Commuter Spends 38 Hours a Year Stuck in Traffic." The Atlantic. Atlantic Media Company, 06 Feb. 2013. Web.*

AS NOT SEEN ON TV ✂

As a native of Long Island and long-time New Yorker, Adam has had trouble getting used to the car-centric culture of Los Angeles. He tries to take advantage of public transportation whenever possible.

Once the roads were gridlocked, the old reliable streetcar became too slow to be effective. And that was the death of public transportation in America.

WE REBUILT CITIES TO COMPENSATE FOR CARS

Once cars became the only way to get from place to place, we rebuilt our entire cities around them. *Source: Yu, Alan. "Study: Hartford, New Haven Hurt By Abundance of Parking." WNPR News. WNPR. Connecticut, 31 Mar. 2014. Study: Hartford, New Haven Hurt By Abundance of Parking. Web.*

That's when things really took a turn for the worse. We started bulldozing entire neighborhoods to build urban highways. In some cities, parking lots now take up a quarter of all the available land. All this space gets used to store cars while they're asleep.

DONALD SHOUP,

Distinguished Professor of Urban Planning at the University of California, Los Angeles:

"Parking lots are deserts in the city. Parking lots don't employ any people. They simply provide space for cars. We have expensive housing for people and free parking for cars. We have our priorities the wrong way around.

"And the worst part is, many cities require far too much parking, and this blights their downtown areas. We're killing our own cities. It's a huge bummer."

THE SCOURGE OF TRAFFIC

The average driver spends one workweek a year stuck in traffic.

Source: Forsyth, Jim. "U.S. Commuters on Average Spend Nearly a Week Stuck in Traffic." Reuters. Thomson Reuters, 05 Feb. 2013. Web.

It's a concept called "induced demand." Historically, every time we've built more roads, the amount of traffic has gone up by an identical amount. We  can't build our way out of the traffic problem. Cars equal traffic, period. *Source: Mann, Adam. "What's Up With That: Building Bigger Roads Actually Makes Traffic Worse" Wired. Conde Nast, 17 June 2014. Web.*

CARS ARE INHERENTLY UNSAFE

- 90 percent of drivers say they're better than average. *Source: Svenson, Ola. "Are We All Less Risky and More Skillful Than Our Fellow Drivers?" Acta Psychologica 47 (1981): 143-48. Web.*

- People who think that they're good drivers are actually the worst drivers.

- Most accidents are caused by inattention. You pay the least amount of attention to the road when you're confident. Which is also why most accidents are caused on clear sunny roads, and to sober drivers. *Source: Vanderbilt, Tom. Traffic: Why We Drive the Way We Do (and What It Says about Us). New York: Alfred A. Knopf, 2008. Print.*

- Studies have shown that modern cars and roads that make us feel secure cause us to unconsciously compensate and drive more dangerously. It's a concept called "risk homeostasis." *Source: Wilde, Gerald JS. "Risk Homeostasis Theory: An Overview." Injury Prevention 4 (1998): 89-91. National Institute of Health. National Institute of Health. Web.*

CARS DON'T REALLY PROVIDE ANY FREEDOM

- The average car costs 9,000 dollars a year just to own. *Source: Stepp, Erin. "Cost of Owning and Operating Vehicle in U.S. Increases Nearly Two Percent According to AAA's 2013 'Your Driving Costs' Study | AAA NewsRoom." AAA NewsRoom. AAA, 15 Apr. 2013. Web.*

- The average American family spends 20 percent of their income on transportation. That's more than they spend on food. And for the poorest Americans, it's 32 percent. *Source: United States. U.S. Bureau of Labor Statistics. BLS Reports: Consumer Expenditures in 2012. N.p.: U.S. Bureau of Labor Statistics, n.d. Web. Report 1046.*

TIM PETERS,

Executive Director of Door of Hope, an organization that helps homeless families go from homelessness to self-sufficiency, to permanent housing and everything in-between:

"Transportation is a big issue with our families. Car ownership can actually set them backwards. We had one client that was paying over 80 percent of her income on a car. She thought it was more important to have a car than a home, because if she ended up homeless, at least she had a car to sleep in—that had been her experience before coming to Door of Hope. Families need a car just to get to work, or to be able to get around in the city. But sometimes, to make a car payment, they'll sacrifice their rent payment, food, or even the basic essentials for their children."

BUT DON'T GIVE UP HOPE

SELETA REYNOLDS,

**General Manager, Los Angeles
Department of Transportation:**

"People say nobody walks in LA, but nothing could be further from the truth. We have one of the busiest rail lines in the country, one of the busiest bus lines in the country, and more people walking and biking every day.

"[LA] community leaders got together and decided that they wanted a place to gather, to create a true public space. It turns out, when you make a great place to walk, it's really good for local businesses. So sometimes, even though it's controversial, we have to take space for streets and give it to people so that everybody has a great choice for how they get around."

some heroes wear glasses

He's about
to drop some
knowledge

WHAT CAN YOU DO?

Cars, of course, can still be fun to drive. And considering the way modern cities have been designed, redesigned, or rebuilt, you may simply need a car. And that's OK. They're a great option for certain kinds of travel. But maybe we should be thinking about cars more like roller blades. They're a lot of fun when you're the only one using them. But, it would really suck if that was the only way people could get to work. So, heck, keep your car, but also use public transportation and support walkability initiatives.

H...
to drop some
knowledge

EPISODE FOUR

ADAM RUINS
FORENSIC
SCIENCE

DIRECTOR: TIM WILKIME
ORIGINAL AIR DATE: OCTOBER 20, 2015

In this episode, Adam reveals the truth about the junk science behind the forensics used in both obnoxious police procedurals and real life—which sometimes gets innocent people sent to jail.

POLICE PROCEDURALS ARE A CRIME AGAINST SCIENCE AND LOGIC

And they're all titled crap like this:

Or *CSI: Cityname* and *SVU: Horriblecrime.* You know the drill. They're dumb, wrong, and wildly misrepresent the subject matter. What's terrible for humanity—i.e., you—is that, due to their popularity, people tend to think cop shows are accurate or educational in some way. As such, there are a lot of inaccuracies that have been absorbed into the public consciousness.

First up?

POLYGRAPH TESTS

The polygraph—lie detector—test is 100 percent old timey pseudoscience. It's akin to what they did in the Dark Ages, where they'd force criminals to hold a red-hot iron to see if it burned them. If it did, it meant you were lying. *Source: Trovillo, Paul V. "History of Lie Detection." Journal of Criminal Law and Criminology 29.6 (1939): 848-81. Northwestern University School of Law Scholarly Commons. Web.*

You can guess how often the "law enforcement" of the time "got their man"—so to speak.

But the modern polygraph is just as ridiculous. Humans are complicated. The truth isn't something you can detect with a machine.

Truthful people can fail polygraphs simply because they're sweaty or nervous. And all you have to do to beat the test is stay cool and keep your heart rate down. Criminals do it all the time.

Here are three psychopaths who beat it:

•Gary Ridgeway, the Green River Killer. *Source: "The Curious Story of How the Lie Detector Came to Be." BBC News. The BBC, 21 May 2013. Web.*

•Soviet spy Aldrich Ames.

•Serial killer Charles Cullen, also known as The Angel of Death. *Source: "Pretending To Be A 'Good Nurse,' Serial Killer Targeted Patients." Fresh Air. WHYY, Philadelphia, Pennsylvania, 15 Apr. 2013. Radio.*

Even the guy who created the damn thing knew it was crap.

JOHN LARSON

as portrayed by Adam Lustick

The polygraph was invented in 1921 by a medical student named John Larson. He would go on to regret inventing it. Larson became so horrified by law enforcement's unscientific use of his device, he would go on to call the machine a "Frankenstein's monster." *Source: Adler, Ken. The Lie Detectors: The History of an American Obsession. New York: Free Press, 2007. Print.*

But no one listened. And ever since, people have insisted that the polygraph can do impossible things. *Source: Eells, Josh. "The Lives They Lived." The New York Times Magazine. The New York Times Company, 21 Dec. 2013. Web.*

In 1966, a polygraph expert named Cleve Backster of the Backster School of Lie Detection conducted tests on plants and concluded that plants have emotions. Instead of the more obvious conclusion, that the machine is a piece of garbage that goes off randomly.

SO WHY DO PEOPLE TRUST IT?

Gee-whiz. Why indeed?

It's because the media—your daytime talk show sleazefests, police procedurals, and cable pundits—has pushed the infallibility of the lie detector so hard that now everyone believes in it, even though it just straight up doesn't work.

Not good. Worse, it's embedded in the American legal system.

Massachusetts uses it to establish probable cause. Florida requires sex offenders to take the test. *Source: Florida Criminal Procedures and Corrections, §948-30 (2012). Web.*

Combined, government agencies test over 70,000 people a year with this century-old piece of pseudo-science. *Source: Stromberg, Joseph. "Lie Detectors: Why They Don't Work, and Why Police Use Them Anyway." Vox. Vox Media, 15 Dec. 2014. Web.*

Do the police know this?

Uh. Yeah. That's not much of a head scratcher.

What is a head scratcher is law enforcement's reliance on eyewitness testimony because....

EYEWITNESS TESTIMONY IS COMPLETELY UNRELIABLE

Much like the plot to a sci-fi novel from the '70s, no, you can't trust your memory. It isn't infallible.

We think of our memories as perfect recordings. But the fact is, even your most cherished childhood recollections are just garbled stories your brain is telling itself.

How do they get so twisted up?

It can go a little like this:

- Every time you tell a story—recall a memory—you add a detail.

- Sometimes when you tell the story, you fit it to cater to different audiences.

- Over time, the memory itself changes.

This isn't because you're lying. It's because that's what brains do. They add details to fill in the gaps.

But don't take our word for it. Let's bring in the expert!

ELIZABETH LOFTUS,

Professor at UC Irvine and a Pioneering Researcher in the Field of False Memories:

"We really need to keep in mind that when people recall something, they can have a lot of detail, a lot of confidence, a lot of emotion when they tell you a story, even though it never happened.

"[Memory] works more like a Wikipedia page, which means you can go in there and edit it, but so can other people. And this has real consequences for law enforcement, because sometimes police, maybe inadvertently, will ask leading or suggestive questions and they can contaminate the memories of the witnesses they're interviewing."

BUT WAIT, IT GETS WORSE!

Even when they don't do it intentionally, cops unconsciously bias and alter the memories of witnesses all the time. *Source: "Eyewitness Identification Reform." The Innocence Project. 10 June 2015. Web*

Know how fingerprints are presented as 100 percent, "no two are alike" evidence?

Yeah, that's never been proven.

Entertaining side fact: In the '80s, a researcher actually found two snowflakes that had precisely the same pattern. *Source: Gopnik, Adam. "All Alike." The New Yorker. Conde Nast, 3 Jan. 2011. Web.*

Neat, right?

Anyway, the "no two fingerprints are alike" cliché isn't science. It's just something one guy named Sir Francis Galton said in 1892.

Uh, just imagine some wonky balding British doof muttering crap like: "My name is Sir Francis Galton. I postulate the chances of two specific individuals having the same fingerprint is very teeny-tiny."

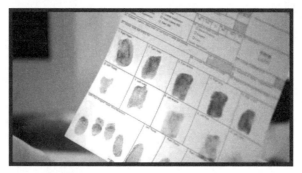

You know, he sounds like a jerk.

And this is a guy who claims to invent eugenics, too, so....

The issue for us now is that Galton's hunch has led everyone to assume that fingerprint evidence is infallible. It ain't.

Case in point: Brandon Mayfield. *Source: "The Real CSI." Frontline. PBS. WGBH, Boston, Massachusetts, 17 Apr. 2012. PBS. Web.*

Mayfield was arrested for the 2004 Madrid, Spain, train bombings after the world's top fingerprint experts swore that he was a perfect match for a print found at the scene.

Thing is, it wasn't Mayfield. Mayfield was an attorney from Oregon who'd never even been to Spain.

Regardless, the FBI arrested Mayfield and held him for weeks. And even after making this mistake, federal agents still maintained that fingerprint evidence was "infallible."

In reality, fingerprint examination is as vulnerable to human error as eyewitness testimony. Because *in reality*, it's not a bunch of cops hobbled around amazing supercomputers. It's more like this:

A lady sitting behind a desk with a magnifying glass eyeballing smudged prints.

Fingerprints pulled from crime scenes tend to be incomplete. And the final stage of matching isn't done by computers—it's done by humans.

That means there's a huge potential for error and bias. It's been shown that analysts can unconsciously change their evaluations, depending on the details of a case. *Source: Russell, Sue. "Bias and the Big Fingerprint Dust-Up." Pacific Standard. 18 June 2012. Web.*

Turns out, there hasn't been much research done regarding how reliable fingerprint analysis actually is.

SIMON COLE,

Criminologist, UC Irvine
Studies Fingerprint Analysis:

"You know, fingerprint evidence has been used in court for over a century now. And until recently, almost no research was done into how reliable it is.

"The Supreme Court ruled in the Dalbert Decision that scientific evidence used in court has to be reliable. According to that decision, unless fingerprint evidence is offered with a substantial proviso, it shouldn't even be allowed in court."

FORENSIC SCIENCE IS KINDA CRAP

Cop shows present forensic science as infallible. But in reality, a lot of it isn't scientific at all. The FBI recently admitted that when conducting hair strand matches, their experts gave flawed testimony in 90 percent of the cases they reviewed. And in death penalty cases, the number was 94 percent, including one time that a hair strand matched to a human turned out to be dog hair. *Source: United States. Federal Bureau of Investigation. The FBI. U.S. Government, 20 Apr. 2015. Web.*

Bite mark analysis is notorious nonsense, promulgated by a small, ungoverned group of dentists. Two men were once sent to death row because of bite marks that were likely made by crawfish. *Source: "2 Men Freed in Child Death Bite-mark Cases." Msnbc.com. NBC News, 29 Feb. 2008. Web.*

AS NOT SEEN ON TV

This was the first genre parody episode, a departure from the show's usual formula. It was a lot of fun, and allowed the creative staff to be playful about riffing on tropes in crime investigation series.

And you've heard how fire investigators "detect" arson by searching for "pouring patterns?"

Scientists have since shown that those patterns happen in any fire that has a flashover event. Eyeballing crime scenes just isn't scientific. *Source: Grann, David. "Trial by Fire." The New Yorker. Conde Nast, 7 Sept. 2009. Web.*

The problem is that these techniques are great at locking people up—but they're terrible at figuring out what actually happened. And that means they often get the wrong person sent to prison, or even executed. Bad forensic science ruins lives and kills people.

DON'T DESPAIR

There is one form of forensic science that works, and it was developed by scientists.

Chris Fabricant can tell you the rest.

CHRIS FABRICANT,
Director, Strategic Litigation Innocence Project:

"DNA evidence was actually developed in a laboratory by scientists rather than police officers in lab coats pretending to be scientists. Real research was done before it was introduced into criminal trials.

"The Innocence Project had a client named Ray Krone who was a regular at a bar in Tucson, Arizona. And the bartender where he used to drink was murdered one night. They had no suspects, no witnesses, and they used bite mark analysis to associate him with that dead body.

"And that was the only evidence that connected him to that crime. He spent ten years on Death Row before DNA evidence exonerated him.

"If we want to continue to throw everybody in prison, then the old technique's just fine. If we want to catch the actual perpetrator, we need to stop using outdated techniques."

If using police resources to educate people is a crime, well, lock us up.

Wait, don't actually do that.

EPISODE FIVE

ADAM RUINS
RESTAURANTS

DIRECTOR: TIM WILKIME
ORIGINAL AIR DATE: OCTOBER 27, 2015

In this episode, Adam uncovers the hidden truths of dining out, including why tipping sucks, the fact that experts can't tell the difference between cheap and expensive wine, and why seafood fraud is rampant in the restaurant industry.

Get ready for some fine dining—with a side of truth.

TIPPING NEEDS TO GO

Declaring tipping to be a crummy practice probably raises more eyebrows than some of Adam's other targets, but hear us out. By the end of this spiel, you'll agree we should do away with tipping.

And let's get one thing straight: If you live in America, you have to tip.

Restaurants in the U.S. can legally pay their servers less than minimum wage—as little as three dollars an hour. *Source: United States. Department of Labor. Wage and Hour Division (WHD): Minimum Wages for Tipped Employees. Washington D.C.: U.S. Department of Labor, 2015. Web.*

As long as that's true, if you don't tip, you're a bad person.

However, just because that's the system we *have* doesn't mean it's a *good* system. Restaurant tipping is a custom that short changes servers, inconveniences customers, and makes the dining experience worse for everyone.

Ask yourself this. Why is it our responsibility to pay the restaurant's employees fairly? Like, why don't they just pay employees a normal amount of money and make the food more expensive? That's what every business has done since the dawn of time.

When you buy a shirt, it's just fifty dollars. They're not like, "OK, that's forty dollars and you decide if the stock boy eats tonight."

In most countries, restaurant tipping isn't mandatory. And even in America, it's a relatively new custom. For most of our history, tipping was considered an undemocratic form of bribery. *Source: Segrave, Kerry. Tipping: An American Social History of Gratuities. Jefferson, NC: McFarland, 1998. Print.*

But after Prohibition banned the sale of alcohol, restaurant profits cratered, and restaurant owners started encouraging servers to accept tips because it meant they could pay them less.

A century later, we're still stuck with the same system, turning what used to be a bribe into an obligation that makes the end of every meal suck.

Unless, of course, your idea of a good time is bickering with your friends about math.

BETTER SERVICE DOESN'T MEAN BETTER TIPS

Research shows that only 2 percent of the difference in tips left by different parties is explainable by the quality in service. In other words, no matter how good of a job you do, you'll be tipped about the same. *Source: Lynn, Michael. "Restaurant Tipping and Service Quality: A Tenuous Relationship." Cornell University School of Hotel Administration The Scholarly Commons 42.1 (2001): 14-20. Web.*

And the worst part is, tipping results in wage discrimination. The research also shows that black servers are tipped less than white servers across the board. *Source: Brewster, Zachary W., and Michael Lynn. "Black–White Earnings Gap among Restaurant Servers: A Replication, Extension, and Exploration of Consumer Racial Discrimination in Tipping." Sociological Inquiry 84.4 (2014): 545-69. Web.*

Considering that racially discriminatory pay is against the law, it's kinda surprising that this entire system isn't straight up illegal. *Source: United States. U.S. Equal Employment Opportunity Commission. U.S. Equal Employment Opportunity Commission. U.S. Government, n.d. Web.*

While patrons don't have much hope of changing the restaurant industry themselves, some restaurants are taking steps to abolish tipping. *Source: Cohen, Patricia. "As Minimum Wages Rise, Restaurants Say No to Tips, Yes to Higher Prices." The New York Times. The New York Times Company, 23 Aug. 2015. Web.*

Restaurants like Brand 158 in Glendale, California.

AS NOT SEEN ON TV ✂

Since this episode aired, there's been a growing number of restaurants paying servers a living wage and eliminating tipping, as well as a swelling movement to pay food service workers fifteen dollars an hour. It's exciting when the show gets to contribute to policy conversations, or make issues more accessible to people who wouldn't seek out wonkier sources. So many of the issues Adam explores on his show evolve in important ways after each episode ends, which perhaps leaves the door open for updates in the future!

GABRIEL FREM,

(left) Owner, Brand 158

CHRISTY KURIAKOSE,

(right) Server, Brand 158

Gabriel Frem: "At Brand 158, we instituted a no tipping policy. And that's been a great success. For our guests, they feel like they're in a nurturing environment where they can relax and enjoy their meal and not have to worry about doing math at the end of the meal to figure out what to tip.

"And, for our servers, it creates stable income so that they can focus on our guests. We don't do it because we feel charitable, we do it because it's good business to take care of your people so that they can take care of your customers like any other business."

And what does the staff think?

Christy Kuriakose: "Oh, the employees love it. Let me tell you, as a server, the fact that I have a stable income is absolutely fantastic. I even have benefits."

GÖRING TOO FAR

Before you saddle up to the bar for some shots of Jägermeister, consider this: Jägermeister is named after Hermann Göring's Huntmasters, or Jägermeisters, of the Nazi era. *Source: Usborne, Simon. "How Jägermeister changed the way we drink." The Independent. Independent Digital News and Media, 20 Apr. 2013. Web.*

Happy drinking!

"CRAFT" ALCOHOL IS GENERALLY NONSENSE

More often than not, there's little difference between the hooch that costs fifteen dollars a pop in a restaurant, and bottom shelf "Crap Brand" bourbon.

It's the same whiskey. Many supposedly "small" batched bourbons and ryes are just the same liquor slightly changed with a cooler label. *Source: "Why Your 'Small-Batch' Whiskey Might Taste A Lot Like The Others." The Salt. NPR, Washington D.C., 30 July 2014. NPR. Web.*

And most popular craft beers are actually brewed by giant corporations. The term is totally unregulated and can be used by anyone. *Source: Tuttle, Brad. "That Craft Beer You're Drinking Isn't Craft Beer. Do You Care?" Time Magazine. Time Inc., 13 Aug. 2013. Web.*

Don't be fooled. Just drink what you like.

DON'T BE A WINER

Feel like you have no idea what you're doing when you order wine?

You're not alone.

Since we can't taste the wines before we buy them, we're forced to pick just based on the label. And even when we do taste them, we doubt our own opinions. So, we defer to the opinions of so-called wine experts.

But the truth is, everyone is pretending.

Here's the big secret: Wine experts can't tell the difference, either. *Source: Dubner, Stephen J. "Do More Expensive Wines Taste Better?" Freakonomics. WNYC, New York, New York, 16 Dec. 2010. Radio.*

Fredric Brochet of the University of Bordeaux conducted a series of tests on unsuspecting wine experts. *Source: McRaney, David. "'You Are Not So Smart': Why We Can't Tell Good Wine From Bad." The Atlantic. Atlantic Media Company, 28 Oct. 2011. Web.*

In another test, experts were asked to compare two different bottles. One, an expensive Grand Cru, and the other, a cheap table wine. Brochet just put the same wine in two different bottles and none of the so-called "wine experts" even noticed.

We say again: Drink what you like.

FUN FACT

DID YOU KNOW THAT LOBSTER WAS ORIGINALLY CONSIDERED FOOD FOR THE POOR? IT DIDN'T BECOME ASSOCIATED WITH WEALTH AND LUXURY UNTIL WWII, WHEN FOOD RATIONING CAUSED SHORTAGES.

Source: Luzer, Daniel. "How Lobster Got Fancy." Pacific Standard. The Miller-McCune Center for Research, Media and Public Policy, 7 June 2013. Web.

SEE FOOD

This is sort of the worst thing. Which, we'll admit, is like being a slightly shinier turd than other turds, given how all this is going.

But.

The awful truth about restaurants is that often, the food you order isn't the food you get. Especially when it comes to seafood.

People who enjoy salmon at restaurants think it's supposed to be a "healthy" pink.

Not so much.

Nearly all farmed salmon starts out a sickly gray color and is dyed pink. *Source: Guilford, Gwynn. "The Costliest Part of Feeding Farmed Salmon: A Pill That Turns Them Pink." The Atlantic. Atlantic Media Company, 15 Mar. 2015. Web.*

In the ocean, wild salmon turned pink because they eat krill. But farmed salmon are fed kibble made of chicken fat, soybeans, and ground up feathers.

Manufacturers then dye the fish pink to make it more appetizing to unwitting consumers.

The fun thing is, salmon would actually be a lot cheaper if it weren't dyed—but we just gotta have pink fish.

And even when the menu says "wild salmon," a lot of the time you're getting farmed salmon and you just don't know it. *Source: Burros, Marian. "Stores Say Wild Salmon, but Tests Say Farm Bred." The New York Times. The New York Times Company, 10 Apr. 2005. Web.*

Maybe you're thinking you'll go with tuna instead. Fair, and a reasonable reaction. But you probably aren't getting real tuna, either.

The mislabeling of fish is rampant in the restaurant industry. A study by Oceana found that 59 percent of the tuna they genetically tested from grocery stores and restaurants wasn't tuna at all. In sushi restaurants, the number was 74 percent. *Source: Mims, Christopher. "59% of the 'Tuna' Americans Eat Is Not Tuna." The Atlantic. Atlantic Media Company, 22 Feb. 2013. Web.*

So, what is that thing you're eating that's not tuna?

Usually, it's a snake mackerel called escolar. And escolar tastes great. You'll be fine…for a few hours. But the flesh of escolar contains waxy deposits that are not easy to digest. *Source: Mims, Christopher. "59% of the 'Tuna' Americans Eat Is Not Tuna." The Atlantic. Atlantic Media Company, 22 Feb. 2013. Web.*

If you haven't made friends with your toilet yet, you soon will.

You might ask yourself: Is this legal? Not really. But it's hard to track down the guilty.

What is legal is the renaming of so-called "trash" fish.

The orange roughy you're eating? Probably tastes decent.

But we don't know if you'd find it quite as flavorful when it was called "the slimehead" by fishermen. *Source: Fahrenthold, David A. "Tastier Names Trouble for Seafood Stocks." The Washington Post. The Washington Post Company, 31 July 2013. Web.*

HERE'S THE THING

Popular species have been so depleted that fishermen have resorted to giving more appetizing names to weird-ass fish that used to be considered too gross to eat.

Here's Adam's dad with more.

DAVID CONOVER,

Marine Biologist, Stony Brook University:

David Conover: "Our recent study showed that 58 percent of the world's fish docks are either overfished or collapsed."

Can anything be done?

David Conover: "Yeah, with respect to overfishing, we need to reduce the amount of fish we're harvesting. We need to make sure that the fish species that are being over harvested are exempt from harvesting until they recover. It's all part of what we call ecosystem-based management."

How does that lead to mislabeling?

David Conover: "When the most popular fish are depleted, the fishing industry has to find new species to harvest. There's thousands of fish in the sea that we serve for food, but the public knows the names of only a few of those fish. So, mislabeling is the obvious result."

LET'S REMEMBER WHERE RESTAURANTS CAME FROM— AND ENJOY THE ILLUSION

In France, after the Revolution toppled the aristocracy, rich folks' personal chefs had nowhere to work, so they opened fine dining restaurants so that even the common man could eat like a king for a day. *Source: Bramen, Lisa. "When Food Changed History: The French Revolution." Smithsonian.com. Smithsonian Institution, 14 July 2010. Web.*

Now, none of us are kings. Or queens. Or, at least, it's *unlikely* that any of us are.

But as long as you don't take the illusion too seriously, or exploit the people who are serving you, it's fine. We just need to all remember that we created this miniature world, so we can change it however we want. If we leave the bad parts and keep the good parts, we'll all have a better time.

EPISODE SIX

ADAM RUINS

HYGIENE

DIRECTOR: TIM WILKIME
ORIGINAL AIR DATE: NOVEMBER 3, 2015

It's time to learn the filthy secrets lurking in our bathrooms, including how ad campaigns make us insecure about our breath, why flushable wipes aren't really flushable, how running water is a miracle of the modern age, and more.

Nobody likes to be stinky. Well, maybe some do, but nobody really likes being around stinky people. You know, that horrible stench of feet and old ashtrays. It's gross.

So, it's no surprise that there's a massive, billion-dollar industry designed around combating human beings' natural stink capabilities.

The issue is that through advertising that makes us feel insecure, the industry has been taking advantage of us for a long time so they can pad their coffers.

Yep. It's true. Your bathroom is chock full of lies.

YOU'RE WASHING YOUR MOUTH WITH FLOOR CLEANER

One hundred years ago, Listerine was used and marketed as a generic household cleaning fluid. *Source: United States. National Institute of Health. Listerine: Past, Present and Future—a Test of Thyme. By DH Fine. Vol. 38. N.p.: Journal of Dentistry, 2010. Web.*

It wasn't until the '20s that Listerine started marketing itself as a way to prevent bad breath. There was just one problem though: Most people thought their breath smelled fine already.

So frustrating for Listerine, right? They devised a plan. They dug up an obscure Latin word and told people it was a disease they could have without even knowing it. *Source: Marchand, Roland. Advertising the American Dream: Making Way for Modernity, 1920-1940. Berkeley: U of California, 1985. Print.*

"Halitosis" is that word. It's Latin for, effectively, mouth disease.

On their own website, Listerine says, "Listerine coined the term 'halitosis.'" Listerine went on to cruelly exploit our insecurities for decades. *Source: "The Listerine Story." Listerine. Johnson & Johnson Limited, n.d. Web.*

They ran ads that said: "Are you unpopular with your own children?"

Or: "Often a bridesmaid, but never a bride!"

Or: "Don't fool yourself. Since halitosis never announces itself to the victim, you simply cannot know when you have it. They talk about you behind your back."

They were really, really successful. After this campaign, Listerine's profits rose 4,000 percent in just seven years. *Source: Marchand, Roland. Advertising the American Dream: Making Way for Modernity, 1920-1940. Berkeley: U of California, 1985. Print.*

AIN'T JUST MOUTHWASH

Advertising based on shame and fear soon became known as the "halitosis style." And the same thing happened with soap. People used to bathe just once a week before the soap industry got to work on them.

Soap companies poured a fortune into advertising the idea that you had to bathe or shower every day. And by the '80s, 90 percent of Americans were doing it.

Source: Vinikas, Vincent. Soft Soap, Hard Sell: American Hygiene in an Age of Advertisement. Ames: Iowa State UP, 1992. Print.

But showering every day isn't necessarily the right course for folks. In fact, it might be bad.

Mileage will vary, but ask your dermatologist.

DR. SARA WARD, MD,
Dermatologist

Do I need to shower every day?

Dr. Sara Ward : "No, in fact, over-showering can dry out your skin because it removes protective lipids and oils. Rinsing off is fine, but you should only use a minimal amount of soap in your underarms and groin. Our skin does actually does a pretty good job of keeping itself clean."

Really?

Dr. Sara Ward: "Yeah."

We are the victims of a generations-long advertising campaign.

Advertisers have spent a century telling us our bodies are disgusting. And now we can't get it out of our heads.

THOSE "FLUSHABLE" WIPES ARE ... BAD

Toilet paper as we know it was invented in 1883. And for the next 118 years, our bottom hygiene routine was pretty simple. Toilet, TP, and wash your hands. And it worked. Those were some of our best hygiene years ever. *Source: United States. CDC. History of Drinking Water Treatment, 30 July 1999. Web.*

Rates of poop-related diseases plummeted during the twentieth century.

Good job, America. Your butts are clean.

Butt (har har) that wasn't good enough.

In 2001, America's paper companies decided to go a sheet further.

The Kimberly Clark Corporation spent 140 million dollars to develop and market the first "flushable" wipes. *Source: Barnes, Julian E. "Kimberly-Clark to Sell Moistened Toilet Paper." The New York Times. The New York Times Company, 17 Jan. 2001. Web.*

And by now you can guess what their pitch was. They told you: You stinky and you just don't know it.

Once again, this shame scam worked. Flushable wipes are now an industry that's worth more than 300 million dollars. And it's no wonder they're trying to shove wipes up our butts. Flushable wipes cost more than six times as much as toilet paper. And these companies would have you use both.

For those thinking there's no-harm, no-foul, "flushable wipes" are ...not flushable. *Source: Goldman, Henry. "Flush-Defying Wipes Bedevil Cities as Sewers Surrender." Bloomberg Business. Bloomberg LP., 7 Sept. 2014. Web.*

"FLUSHABLE" ... ANYTHING

Toilet paper breaks down almost instantly in water. Flushable wipes don't.

And while a lot of things technically *can* go down the toilet. That doesn't mean they should.

We're creating "fatbergs" with our own need to be "clean."

It's a strange, disgusting blob of discarded... everything. It's squishy and rank and pale. It has the unfortunate consistency of thick, rotted Crisco shortening.

And we're building them in our sewage system.

Congealed masses of flushable wipes combined with cooking oil and other junk.

TYRONE JUE,
San Francisco Public Utility Commission:

"Everything you flush down the toilet, we have to deal with. In San Francisco, we've had to spend about 4 million dollars a year having to clear out these fatbergs. Every city across the world is dealing with exactly the same problem.

"Even if flushable wipes make your butt feel a little cleaner, they're murder on our sewers."

And it's not just wipes. Things like exfoliating microbeads, antibacterial soaps, and unused medications, all go down our drains.

Source: Donn, Jeff, Martha Mendoza, and Justin Pritchard. "PHARMAWATER II Fish, Wildlife Affected by Drug Contamination in Water." Associated Press. 10 Mar. 2008. Web.

DON'T DESPAIR

Your shower is...pretty much all you need.

Running water needs to be appreciated. It's a miracle weapon.

The fact that we can summon clean, fresh water on command is the greatest marvel of the modern age.

For most of human history, sanitation was basically nonexistent. Most people just dumped their waste in the streets. Even the rich were gross. *Source: George, Rose. The Big Necessity: The Unmentionable World of Human Waste and Why It Matters. New York: Metropolitan, 2008. Print.*

The nobles of Versailles relieved themselves in the palace hallways. But as cities got bigger and denser, problems started...piling up. By 1858, London was so smelly, it was referred to as "the Great Stink." *Source: Public Health. "Who Eradicated the 'Great Stink of London'"? Washington University at St. Louis, 2015. Web.*

Londoners dumped their waste directly into the River Thames, which was also the source of their drinking water. The inevitable result was a cholera outbreak that killed 50,000 people. Turns out, the #1 poison in human history is our own #2.

In desperation, Parliament ordered engineer Joseph Basiljet to construct the city's first proper sewers. In what was at that time the biggest civil engineering project in history, Basiljet built over 1,100 miles of brick sewers under London. That's the length of almost a million Benedict Cumberbatches. *Source: Halliday, Stephen. The Great Stink of London: Sir Joseph Bazalgette and the Cleansing of the Victorian Metropolis. The History Press, 2013. Print.*

Thanks to Basiljet's heroic poop chute, cholera outbreaks were largely ended and child mortality dropped by a fifth.

And it wasn't just England.

To improve sanitation in Chicago, an engineer named Ellis Chesbrough jacked up entire neighborhoods by as much as fourteen feet. *Source: Young, David. "Raising the Chicago Streets out of the Mud." The Chicago Tribune. Tribune Publishing, 19 Nov. 2013. Web.*

And reversed the flow of the Chicago River, all to protect the Windy City from typhoid. Basiljet and Chesbrough are true heroes.

But because we don't like talking about poop, most of us don't even know their names. Modern sanitation has arguably saved more lives than any other invention in human history. *Source: Childs, Dan and Susan Kansagra. "10 Health Advances That Changed the World." ABC News. ABC News Network, 20 Sept. 2007. Web.*

It turns out video games are right: Plumbers really do save the world.

THE HOLE PROBLEM

While public sanitation is the greatest health advance of the twentieth century, toilets still have one big problem. Not everyone has them yet. While we're taking our porcelain thrones for granted, worldwide 2.5 billion people still have to use unsafe pit toilets. *Source: "International Decade for Action 'Water for Life' 2005-2015." UN News Center. UN, 23 Oct. 2014. Web.*

And another one billion still have to poop in the great outdoors.

Here's Jack Sim from the World Toilet Organization, a global nonprofit dedicated to improving toilet and sanitation conditions worldwide, with more.

Jack Sim: "Lots of people don't have access to a proper toilet. They defecate next to the river and they pollute the water, spreading diseases of diarrhea, killing lots of children every year.

"We shouldn't shut down the conversation. People are just too shy to talk about this subject. And when you don't talk about something, you cannot improve. We have to put serious resources into this agenda."

EPISODE SEVEN

ADAM RUINS
VOTING

DIRECTORS: VINCENT PEONE, JOSH RUBEN
ORIGINAL AIR DATE: NOVEMBER 10, 2015

Ah, the rush to get to the polls. The democratic process. Voting! It's one of America's founding principles. A vote for everyone. We, the people, shaping the future of this great nation.

Can you smell that? Smells like...democracy.

Except....

EVERYTHING YOU KNOW ABOUT VOTING IS WRONG

You probably think your vote counts just as much as anyone else's. Heck, that's what all Americans are taught. But it isn't true.

Some votes count way, way more than others.

As much as we try, and despite our best intentions, our democracy isn't very...democratic.

There are pretty dang serious reasons for that.

THE ELECTORAL COLLEGE

Every four years we hear the words "Electoral College" over and over again, but we never talk about what a ridiculous—and frankly, undemocratic—system it really is. The Electoral College gives vastly more power to different voters, depending on which state they live in.

If you're thinking the bigger states get more bang for their voting buck, you're wrong. It's the smaller states that do. If your state has fewer people, you have more power.

Take Wyoming: Not too many people live in Wyoming, but they have three electoral votes, or one for every 135,000 voters.

Here's California: California is packed with people, but they have fifty-five electoral votes, or one for every 411,000 voters.

And that's totally out of proportion, because it means it takes three times as many Californians to earn one electoral vote, giving voters in Wyoming three times the power in the Electoral College. *Source: Cowan, Sarah K., Stephen Doyle, and Drew Heffron. "Op-Chart: How Much Is Your Vote Worth?" The New York Times. The New York Times Company, 02 Nov. 2008. Web.*

As a result of this system, your vote could count for less just because of where you live.

The real problem, though, is that the Electoral College creates swing states.

SWING STATES

The fact that the entire election is determined by just a handful of states is really messed up. For one thing, it means presidential candidates can ignore almost the entire country.

Swing states have so much power that in recent elections, up to 80 percent of all the votes cast in America had no impact on the outcome. *Source: "Problems with the Electoral College." FairVote. FairVote, 2014. Web.*

And before you go thinking, "Well, there are red states and blue states," we're gonna have to stop you right there.

Most states are actually pretty purple. *Source: Sides, John. "Most Americans Live in Purple America, Not Red or Blue America." The Washington Post. The Washington Post, 12 Nov. 2013. Web.*

In 2012, over three million Texans voted Democrat. And almost five million Californians voted Republican. *Source: United States. U.S. National Archives and Records Administration. Office of the Federal Register. 2012 Presidential Election Popular Vote Totals. College Park, 2012. Web. Source: Howard, Chris. What America Looks Like. 2012. Licensed under Creative Commons Attribution-ShareAlike 3.0 Unported License.*

If electoral votes were awarded proportionately, in 2012, sixteen of Texas's electoral votes would've gone to Barack Obama and twenty of California's would've gone to Mitt Romney. But in our winner-take-all system, anyone who wants to vote for their state's losing party might as well just stay at home.

The Electoral College isn't just a name, either. When we vote, we're actually just picking our state's electors. Then those electors get together and cast their ballots for president.

As for who the electors are, you probably won't be surprised. They're mostly retired politicians and party flaks.

And don't get to thinking that electors "have" to vote for the candidate the voters pick. In twenty-four states, they can vote for whoever they want. *Source: United States. U.S. National Archives and Records Administration. Office of the Federal Register. What Is the Electoral College? State Laws and Requirements. Washington D.C.: U.S. National Archives and Records Administration, 2000. Web.*

And that's happened over eighty times. In 2004, an elector in Minnesota cast his vote for someone named "John Ewards" which was almost the name of the John Kerry's running mate. *Source: Brodarick, Taylor. "It's Time To Abolish The Electoral College." Forbes. Forbes Magazine, 4 Nov. 2012. Web.*

The Electoral College is such a bad system, people have been trying to abolish it for centuries...but so far, it's been politically impossible.

IT'S TRUE, THE FOUNDING FATHERS SCREWED UP

The founding fathers didn't actually think that most Americans should be able to vote. Sucks, but it's true.

ED AYERS,

Historian at the University of Richmond:

Ed Ayers: "We revere the Founding Fathers, as we should. But their ideas of democracy were just a little bit different than ours."

Basically, they didn't entirely trust the average citizens of the new United States of America to vote correctly.

Ed Ayers: "Put yourself in their shoes. They're creating a new country, they're not sure what's gonna happen. They're kind of worried about too much democracy. They think it'd be a good idea maybe if there'd be a buffer between the people and the government."

And they were kind of condescending.

Ed Ayers: "...There was one particular group of states that rallied really hard against direct democracy."

Slave states played a major role in the creation of the Electoral College.

Ed Ayers: "Well, to a considerable extent. Slave states are very powerful. And if you're gonna have a United States, you're gonna have to make concessions to bring them in."

The Founding Fathers weren't benevolent demigods. They were humans who made compromises and mistakes. And building a compromise with slavery into the structure of our government was one of them.

The fact of the matter is, if you didn't own land and/or you were a woman, they didn't think you should have a vote. *Source: United States. National Archives. The Charters of Freedom. Washington D.C.: U.S. National Archives and Records Administration, 2015. Web.*

When the founding fathers created our democracy, they gave the vote to just 6 percent of the population. *Source: United States. National Archives. The Charters of Freedom. Washington D.C.: U.S. National Archives and Records Administration, 2015. Web.*

And it took a long time to change that.

In fact, it took almost seventy years.

A BRIEF HISTORY OF VOTING HISTORY

It was 1856 before the right to vote was extended to include all white men. *Source: "U.S. Voting Rights Timeline." Northern California Citizenship Project. KQED, San Francisco, California, 2004. Web.*

And then fourteen years later, in 1870, the Fifteenth Amendment finally gave black men the right to vote.

Soon after that, in 1889, states passed Jim Crow laws that made it virtually impossible for black Americans to vote.

In 1920, women finally got the franchise.

And forty-five years after that, the Voting Rights Act of 1965 finally secured African Americans' right to vote.

Which brings us to the present.

AND YET IT'S STILL BROKEN

There are still millions of American citizens who pay taxes and don't have representation. Those suffering without suffrage include the citizens of Washington, D.C.

650,000 people live in D.C. and have no representation in Congress. *Source: United States. U.S. Census Bureau. District of Columbia QuickFacts from the US Census Bureau. N.p., 31 Aug. 2015. Web.*

Come on!

And America's territories, like American Samoa, Puerto Rico, and Guam. They're American citizens, geez.

Finally, there are felons. In many states, felons are barred from voting for the rest of their lives. Even after they're released.

VOTING IN THE JIM CROW SOUTH

Ed Ayers: "You know, for one hundred years in the Jim Crow South, white southerners did everything they could to keep black southerners from voting. They would take minor crimes and turn them into felonies, and then pass laws saying that felons can't vote."

A lot of those laws are still on the books, and they're still stopping African Americans from voting. *Source: Bouie, Jamelle. "The Jim Crow Zombie That Won't Die." The Daily Beast. Newsweek/Daily Beast, 11 Feb. 2014. Web.*

DARYL ATKINSON,
Senior Staff Attorney at the Southern Coalition for Social Justice:

Daryl Atkinson: "In 1996, I was convicted of a first-time nonviolent drug crime. I was sentenced to ten years in prison, spent almost four years there.

"And once I got out, I was able to get my education, get my Bachelor's degree, law degree. I'm licensed to practice law in two different states. Been even honored at the White House by the president, but I still can't vote in my home state.

"And this doesn't just affect me. Because African Americans are disproportionately arrested for nonviolent crimes. 13 percent of African-American males in this country can't vote because of felon disenfranchisement laws."

The bottom line is, Jim Crow laws that are still on the books are stopping five million Americans like Daryl from voting every year.

Source: Gonchar, Michael. "Should Felons Be Allowed to Vote After They Have Served Their Time?" The New York Times. The New York Times Company, 18 Feb. 2014. Web.

Maybe you think you can change things with your vote. Go for it! But there's a problem.

THE AMERICAN ELECTION SYSTEM HAS ALWAYS BEEN BROKEN

Thing is, American democracy has never been perfect. Throughout our history, politicians and parties have used undemocratic—often even fraudulent—means to get elected.

In the nineteenth century, people would just sell their votes outright and make bank, traveling from state to state being paid to vote. *Source: Onuf, Peter, Ed Ayers, Brian Balogh, Marc Summers, Alexander Keyssar, and Jamie Raskin. "Pulling the Curtain: Voting in America." Audio blog post. Backstory with the American History Guys. Virginia Foundation for the Humanities, 2 Nov. 2012. Web.*

In fact, election fraud was common practice well into the twentieth century. LBJ won his first Senate election by buying the votes of entire districts, and was finally put over the top when a corrupt election worker changed a seven to a nine.

And things haven't gotten any better.

To this day, political parties pick the winners of elections before they even happen. It's a process called "gerrymandering" and it's totally legal.

Every ten years, politicians redraw the districts that pick the House and State legislatures. But here's the problem: The politicians that are elected by those districts are the same politicians that redraw the districts. *Source: Ingraham, Christopher. This is the best explanation of gerrymandering you will ever see. How to steal an election: a visual guide. Washington Post. Washingtonpost. Newsweek Interactive. 1 March, 2015. Web.*

It's an insane conflict of interest because it allows political parties to choose the outcomes of elections years in advance.

If you think that sounds really, really similar to cheating, that's because it is.

In 2012, Pennsylvania Republicans lost the popular vote. But they still won 72 percent of the seats in their state by drawing weird looking districts. *Source: Prokop, Andrew. "What is gerrymandering?" Vox. Vox Media, 15 May 2014. Web.*

And Maryland Democrats did the exact same thing when they drew their own grotesquely unfair district.

The only other country with a bonkers system like this is…France. *Source: Prokop, Andrew. "How Do Other Countries Handle Redistricting?" Vox. Vox Media, 15 May 2014. Web.*

AS NOT SEEN ON TV

Sometimes viewers quip to Adam or comment online that this episode convinced them that voting is dumb. But that's disappointing, since it contradicts the actual conclusion of the episode. Of course you should vote. Watch the conclusions, guys!

DON'T GIVE UP HOPE

This is all why it's so critically important that people *do* vote.

The Founding Fathers said all men are created equal, and they couldn't live up to it in their era. But they built a machine that allows us to get better every generation. Now it's our turn.

American democracy isn't perfect, but it used to be a lot worse. And our system is actually more inclusive and democratic than it has ever been before. And that's because we've used democracy to make democracy stronger.

If you want things to get better, you have to vote.

Here's one simple idea: Why don't we make Election Day a national holiday? It's way too difficult for busy Americans to get to the polls.

That way, more Americans could vote more easily and we would have time to celebrate Election Day for what it is—the most patriotic day of the year.

EPISODE EIGHT

ADAM RUINS
WORK

DIRECTORS: VINCENT PEONE, JOSH RUBEN
ORIGINAL AIR DATE: NOVEMBER 17, 2015

Guess what? Not only is the American forty-hour workweek exhausting for employees, it can actually *hurt* businesses. And if you're a freelancer or an intern, chances are your employers are illegally taking advantage of you. Possibly the weirdest part? Talking about how much you make with your coworkers is healthy for both you and the workplace. It's true: Work sucks—and we can prove it.

HORRIBLE BOSSES

The "cool boss"? He probably stinks.

There are few things more obnoxious than a boss who thinks it's super fun and cool to dive into your personal life, or a manager who shows some weird desire to be pals with everyone in the office.

It's made even more tiresome when that office is jammed with distractions meant to display that you're breaking your back in a "happy environment."

No number of ping-pong tables and Nerf guns solve some jobs' soul-crushing nature.

A lot of that boils down to....

THE FORTY-HOUR WORKWEEK

If an employee has completed their duties for the day, why the heck can't they leave? Because their job enforces a five-day, forty-hour workweek. But that schedule is an outdated relic that does nothing but exhaust employees and hurt business.

Most of that time is wasted. A recent survey found that employees spent only 45 percent of the workday on primary job duties. *Source: Lam, Bourree. "The Wasted Workday." The Atlantic. Atlantic Media Company, 04 Dec. 2014. Web.*

What do they do with the other 55 percent?

Mostly browse Facebook and go to pointless meetings.

We will say this: It used to be worse. 100 years ago, the average worker clocked ten-hour days six days a week. *Source: Costa, Dora L. "The Wage and Length of the Work Day: From the 1890s to 1991." Papers and Proceedings (1998): 1-44. American Economic Association. Web.*

Back then, most workers rarely had even a single day all to themselves. Luckily, there were two groups that fought for the modern Saturday: labor unions and Jewish people. *Source: Clark, Krissy. "A Weekend History Lesson." Weekend America. American Public Media, St. Paul, Minnesota, 24 Nov. 2007. Web.*

And those two groups had an unlikely ally: the founder of Ford Motor Company, Henry Ford.

In 1926, he gave all his workers two days off a week. This inspired numerous companies to follow suit. Granted, he was also really sure the Jews caused World War 1. *Source: Baldwin, Neil. Henry Ford and the Jews: The Mass Production of Hate. New York: Public Affairs, 2001. Print.*

So....

Anyway, Henry Ford was super racist and he despised labor unions, so he didn't help change the workweek out of love for the workers. He did it for himself.

Overworked employees are less productive. And worse yet, they had no time to buy his stuff.

AS NOT SEEN ON TV ✂

Two notable creative team members had bit parts in this episode: Travis Helwig, the show's head writer, played Peter, and Greg Tuculescu, who played Tom, later became the showrunner for a miniseries of animated episodes that debuted during Season 2.

Ford didn't give an F150 about his employees' leisure time. He helped create Saturday because he knew it would be good for business. And as technology improved and productivity rose, everyone thought the workweek would keep getting shorter. In 1930, the economist John Maynard Keanes predicted:

˙BY 2030, WE WILL BE WORKING FOR AS LITTLE AS FIFTEEN HOURS A WEEK.˙ - JOHN MAYNARD KEYNES

Source: "Economic Possibilities for Our Grandchildren." Essays in Persuasion. New York: W.W.Norton, 1963. 358-73. Keynes on Possibilities. Yale University, 2009. Web.

• • • • • • • • • • •

Even Richard Nixon agreed:

• • • • • • • • • • •

˙THE FOUR-DAY WORKWEEK IS INEVITABLE WITHIN OUR TIME.˙ - RICHARD NIXON

Source: Theis, William. "Nixon Defends 4-Day Week Claim." The Milwaukee Sentinel. 25 Sept. 1956. Web.

And for a while it looked like it might have been right. For decades, work hours steadily decreased. But in the '70s, Americans started working longer and longer hours.

We now work nearly four more weeks a year than we did in 1979. *Source: Mishel, Lawrence. Vast majority of wage earners are working harder, and for not much more. Rep. Economic Policy Institute, 30 Jan. 2013. Web.*

And all those extra hours are actually terrible for your business. Overtime increases the rate of mistakes and safety mishaps among industrial workers by 61 percent. *Source: Dembe, A E, J B Erickson, R G Delbos, and S M Banks. "The Impact of Overtime and Long Work Hours on Occupational Injuries and Illnesses: New Evidence from the United States." Occupational & Environmental Medicine 62.9 (2005): 588-97. BMJ. BMJ Publishing Group Ltd., 8 Mar. 2005. Web.*

And longer hours also lower the scores on cognitive performance tests, which means businesses are literally working their employees stupid. *Source: Virtanen, Marianna, Archana Singh-Manoux, Jane E. Ferrie, David Gimeno, Michael G. Marmot, Marko Elovainio, Markus Jokela, Jussi Vahtera, and Mika Kivimäki. "Long Working Hours and Cognitive Function: The Whitehall II Study." American Journal of Epidemiology 169.5 (2008): 596-605. Oxford Journals. Oxford University Press, 6 Jan. 2009. Web.*

BUT ALL THIS WORK MADE AMERICA THE RICHEST COUNTRY IN THE WORLD!

Nah.

There are plenty of wealthy countries that work far less than we do. Workers in Germany, the strongest economy in Europe, work an average of 400 hours less a year than the average American worker. *Source: "Average Annual Hours Actually Worked per Worker." OECD.Stat. OECD, 2015. Web.*

Do you have any idea how much 400 hours a year is? That's ten full work weeks.

And working long isn't the same thing as working hard. Employees would be happier, healthier, and more productive, if they had more time off.

Don't believe us? Meet Ryan Carson.

RYAN CARSON,

CEO, Treehouse, an Online School:

Ryan Carson: "So yeah, in 2006, we switched to a four-day workweek for our entire company."

And this is good for your business?

Ryan Carson: "So, it just seemed to make a lot of sense. When people come to work well rested, they have more energy and better ideas. We are also able to retain top talent for longer, which saves us a ton of money in the long-term.

"You know, if I'm lucky, I have 2,500 weekends left in my entire life. And with the four-day workweek, I get 50 percent more time with my wife and kids, and that's what's important to me."

American business has changed a ton in the last century, but it still clings to the same schedule used back in Henry Ford's day—out of sheer habit. Even though it hurts business.

OH, DON'T GET US STARTED ON INTERNS

OK, so about interns....

The great American intern. They get our coffee, they make our copies, and sure, they may not be paid, but they receive something far more valuable in return: skills and experience.

Right?

Wrong.

Internships are nothing but a way for companies to exploit young people for free labor, and in many cases, they are totally illegal.

Robert Reich can explain more.

ROBERT REICH,

Secretary of Labor under Bill Clinton:

"According to the Labor Department, internships are only legal if it's for the benefit of the interns, not the company, and the payment isn't just the promise of a job at the end. It doesn't displace any regular employees, and is similar to what you learn in an educational environment." *Source: Hickman, Blair, and Christie Thompson. "When Is It OK to Not Pay an Intern?" ProPublica. ProPublica Inc., 14 June 2013. Web.*

A new study suggests that unpaid interns go on to have nearly exactly the same hiring rate as people who have never interned at all. *Source: National Association of Colleges and Employers. "The Class of 2014 Student Survey Report." NACE. Sep, 2014. Web.*

And since interns aren't paid anything, someone else has to support them while they work for free. It's a disastrous situation.

Heck, people from lower income families can't take internships *at all* because they have to support themselves. They literally cannot afford to work in some cases. That's messed up.

LANCING THE FREELANCERS

Getting shoehorned into a forty-hour workweek without benefits but promised cupcakes on Fridays? Sounds like you got snookered by your company's idea of "freelancing."

ROBERT REICH,
Secretary of Labor under Bill Clinton...again:

"The classification of salaried employees as freelancers is a very common problem in corporate America. A company is probably working you as a freelancer illegally if they: impose requirements over you on shift times, meetings or office attendance, don't give you the freedom to work for other companies, or just generally treat you like staff." *Source: Fallon, Nicole. "Contract Workers vs. Employees: What Businesses Should Know." Business News Daily. Purch, 1 Oct. 2014. Web.*

In 1995, 93 percent of American workers were full-time or part-time staff. *Source: United States. Bureau of Labor Statistics. Monthly Labor Review. Bureau of Labor Statistics, Mar. 2001. Web.*

But today, nearly one in three are freelance or temp. *Source: Weber, Lauren. "One in Three U.S. Workers Is a Freelancer." The Wall Street Journal, 4 Sept. 2014. Web.*

Why do you think that is?

Businesses hire freelancers because they're comparatively cheap.

Bosses love to cut corners. That's why they turn staffers into free-lancers so they don't have to pay for the benefits they're entitled to. By avoiding unemployment, taxes, and Workmen's Compensation healthcare, they save up to 30 percent on wages. *Source: Field, Anne. "The IRS Targets Independent Contractors." Bloomberg Business. Bloomberg L.P., 22 Apr. 2010. Web.*

THE ECONOMY AIN'T CAUSING THESE SHORTCUTS

Even taking the recession into account, American businesses make more money now than ever. Yet wages haven't risen to match, all because companies keep pleading poverty and making sacrifices. *Source: United States. Compensation of Employees: Wages & Salary Accruals/Gross Domestic Product. Economic Research. Federal Reserve Bank of St. Louis, n.d. Web.*

So, tell you what, why don't they skip all the meaningless perks and give freelancers and interns a proper salary with benefits?

Simple: Those meaningless perks are cheaper.

Yay! Capitalism!

If you're concerned about your bottom line, know this: You can't win loyalty with sugar, Nerf, and foosball tables.

Cute crap around the office doesn't matter when your workers can't afford to get their kid's teeth fixed.

TALKING ABOUT YOUR SALARY IS OK—AND EVEN BENEFICIAL

Discussing money in the workplace is generally *verboten*. A big no-no. But there are good reasons to do so. And if your boss tells you that you can't, well—joke's on them—because they're breaking the law. *Source: United States. National Labor Relations Act. National Labor Relations Board, n.d. Web.*

The right to share your salary is protected by the National Labor Relations Act. Employees have the right to engage in open talks about money. And being public with your salary actually benefits them.

Americans have an enormous taboo against talking about money. Most people would rather discuss their sex lives than their salaries.

Which is kind of gross, but that's where we are.

All that taboo does is take power away from the employee and give it to the company.

Bosses love it when you keep your salary a secret because it tilts pay negotiations in their favor. It's a concept called "information asymmetry." If you don't know what the going rate is for your salary, it's easier for the company to rip you off.

This perpetuates the pay gap.

For instance, African-American women make sixty-four cents for every dollar the average white guy makes. *Source: United States. Income, Earnings, and Poverty Data From the 2007 America Community Survey. U.S. Census Bureau. U.S. Department of Commerce, Aug. 2008. Web.*

The bottom line is: If you don't have all the information, you could get scammed big time.

Discussing your salary with your coworkers is your right as an employee. When you let the bosses stop you from doing it, you push your own wages down, which means you're spending more years of your life slaving away at a job that doesn't pay you what you are really worth.

THE REAL BOTTOM LINE

Take care of your team first.

Ryan Carson, Lifetree CEO: "Treating people well really is the best way to do business."

Robert Reich: "And paying employees' low wages and overworking them is bad for capitalism as a whole, because if people don't have time and money to buy things, the economy would grind to a halt. The only way to build a stable, strong economy is making sure the average worker has cash and free time. Take of our team first. Treating people well really is the best way to do business."

ADAM RUINS
SUMMER FUN

DIRECTORS: VINCENT PEONE, JOSH RUBEN
ORIGINAL AIR DATE: DECEMBER 1, 2015

You know the feeling of waking up on summer vacation. It's amazing, for once, to have the sun warm your face. And your heart is filled with excitement about what lies in those whimsical days ahead. Problem is, summer vacation makes you dumber. Even the things kids enjoy during their summer breaks are lousy with deceit. But we'll get into that later.

SUMMER OF LIES

Summer vacation is a blight on our educational system. Thems the breaks. We know everyone, or nearly everyone, has fond memories of *not* having to go to school, but summer break is terrible for kids.

AS NOT SEEN ON TV ✂

Usually the show's writers and researchers pitch segment ideas surrounding a given theme, but this was an example of the opposite. There were three loosely-related segment ideas, and the team brainstormed ways to connect them before settling on "summer fun." The sweet story arc between the brother and sister helped make the episode work well.

Yeah, yeah, we can already hear the children screaming at the very notion that they're supposed to learn during vacation. Except here's the thing: They *are* kids. Learning is their entire job.

So why do our schools stop kids from learning for three whole months?

Everyone says it's so farm kids can do farm things on a farm.

But that ain't true.

JERRY POTTER,

Actual Farmer, Owner, Operator Express Ranch:

"I harvest in the fall. I plant in the spring. I don't do crap in the summer."

The "agrarian" calendar explanation is a total myth. The real reason schools close in the summer is because of the heat. A hundred years ago we didn't have air conditioning.

During the summer, classrooms would become so unbearably hot that rich people pulled their kids out of school for months, taking them to the countryside. *Source: Melker, Saskia De, and Sam Weber. "Agrarian Roots? Think Again. Debunking the Myth of Summer Vacation's Origins." PBS Newshour. PBS, 7 Sept. 2014. Web.*

Yeah. Kids have summer vacations because rich people were hot. And it's making them dumb.

SUMMER BREAK MAKES YOU STUPID

Kids lose an average of one month of instruction every summer. *Source: Cooper, Harris, Barbara Nye, Kelly Charlton, James Lindsay, and Scott Greathouse. "The Effects of Summer Vacation on Achievement Test Scores: A Narrative and Meta-Analytic Review." Review of Educational Research 66.3 (1996): 227-68.Duke University. Duke University, 26 Jan. 2011. Web.*

Educators call it the "summer slide."

It's easy to forget what you learned when you spend three whole months doing nothing but watching TV.

Or, hey, we'll throw you a bone: Maybe you or your kids can go to summer camp and learn some things there. Nice. But it's too expensive for lots of other families.

That's right.

SUMMER BREAK HURTS THE POOR

Summer break is especially hard on the poorest kids because school provides them with lunches they can't get at home.

And help exists, but many kids have trouble accessing summer lunch programs.

How many?

Six out of every seven kids eligible for summer lunch programs never receive them. *Source: "Summer Meals: Summer Meals Survey of Parents." No Kid Hungry, Center for Best Practices. Share Our Strength, n.d. Web.*

TONY BROWN,

Executive Director, Heart of Los Angeles:

Tony Brown: "It's true. Summer's a real problem for the kids I work with...Summer slide is so bad for the low-income kids that we work with every day."

Why?

Tony Brown: "Well, our kids live in really unsafe neighborhoods, so they stay inside in front of the television all summer long."

What do you guys do to help?

Tony Brown: "We provide free summer programs in academics, arts, and athletics, so the kids can stay safe, off the street, and away from gangs. We're doing all we can. But unfortunately, there are still millions of kids who have nowhere to go during the summer."

some heroes wear glasses

so many pocket squares, so little time

In countries like Japan and England, students get multiple short breaks throughout the year. *Source: Lyons, Linda. "Can We Learn From Year-Round Schooling?" 12 November, 2012. Gallup. Web.*

But in our system, we just wash our hands of the neediest kids for three whole months.

But wait! It gets worse!

Even the stuff kids enjoy *watching* on their summer breaks is terrible.

THE DISNEY DISASTER

So, then, you think the kids can enjoy those long summers watching TV? Bad News: The creators and owners of kids favorite shows and characters have seriously messed up our copyright laws.

Ever since his first appearance as Steamboat Willie, kids have loved Mickey Mouse. Back in the '20s, our copyright system worked the way it was supposed to. An artist who created a new work could claim the exclusive right to it for fifty-six years. *Source: The Association of Research Libraries. "Copyright Timeline: A History of Copyright in the United States." ARL. org. 2015. Web.*

Long enough to make a healthy profit for pretty much their entire lifetime. After that, the work entered the public domain, giving every- one the right to copy, share, and use it to create works of their own.

Remixing the works of the past is an essential part of how we cre- ate new culture. And this same process brought us so many of your favorite characters—like Frankenstein, Dracula, Sherlock Holmes, Sleeping Beauty, Alice in Wonderland, the Wizard of Oz, Hercules, Pinocchio, Dr. Jekyll and Mr. Hyde, Captain Nemo, Paul Bunyan, Tarzan, King Arthur, Robin Hood, Moby Dick, and many, many more. *Source: Lessig, Lawrence. Free Culture: How Big Media Uses Technology and the Law to Lock down Culture and Control Creativity. New York: Penguin, 2004. Print.*

All of them were created by artists long ago, and are now in the public domain, free for us to use to tell our own stories. You can make them play soccer or fight a space battle.

These characters now belong to all of us. It's a little something we like to call...The Circle of Rights.

But!

In 1998, Mickey Mouse was about to enter the public domain. To stop that from happening, Disney and other companies lobbied Congress to extend the term of copyright by decades, just so they could retain ownership of him and other characters. *Source: Lee, Timothy B. "15 years ago, Congress kept Mickey Mouse out of the public domain. Will they do it again?" Washingtonpost.com. Washingtonpost. Newsweek Interactive. 25 Oct. 2013. Web.*

Now, all those characters that would belong to us, belong to them.

This problem is far more serious than just cartoons.

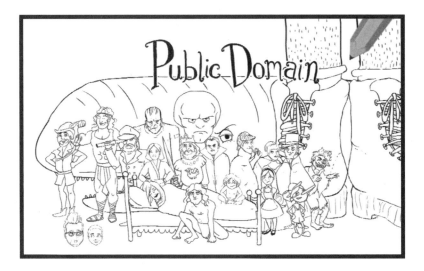

JAMES BOYLE,

Co-founder of the Center for Public Domain at Duke University:

James Boyle: "Because of these laws, nothing's entered the public domain for years. In fact, no published work went to the public domain until 2019: Books, songs, movies, and even scientific articles, are stuck in a legal limbo."

This leads to "orphaned works."

James Boyle: "They're under copyright, but their original owners can't be found. It's illegal to share them, but they got share themselves so they're trapped down here in intellectual property purgatory."

There could be any number of great works in there, but we'll never know thanks to copyright extension.

James Boyle: "Until the last fifty years, every generation in American history has had free and legal access to the creativity of the past. They could learn from it. They could build on it. Now, all that creativity is locked away."

And the true irony is that no one understood that better than Walt Disney. Dozens of Disney characters were taken directly from the public domain. *Source: Khanna, Derek. "50 Disney Movies Based On The Public Domain." Forbes. Forbes Magazine, 3 Feb. 2014. Web.*

Even the breakthrough Mickey cartoon "Steamboat Willie" is based on a Buster Keaton movie from 1928 called *Steamboat Bill Jr*.

Disney cartoons are fun to watch, but they're made by a company that profits from our shared cultural heritage while refusing to contribute to it. That really stinks.

So, if you can't relax and enjoy Disney cartoons on your summer vacation...maybe you can enjoy video games?

VIDEO GAMES GOT PROBLEMS, PLAYA

Mostly in the gender arena. Specifically, the fact that our gendered cultural attitudes towards video games are destroying the medium.

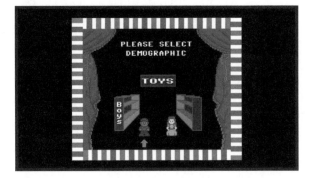

You've heard this more than you want to: "Video games are for boys."

This is wrong and dumb.

But still, to most people, video games are as male as the color blue.

Except even *that* is wrong.

A LITTLE HISTORY

Guess this child's gender:

If you thought female, you'd be wrong.

That's actually how our thirty-second president, Franklin Delano Roosevelt, dressed as a child.

Before WWII, little boys and little girls wore the same outfits—pretty dresses. *Source: Maglaty, Jeanna. "When Did Girls Start Wearing Pink?" Smithsonian. com. Smithsonian Institution, 7 Apr. 2011. Web.*

In the '50s, gender-specific clothing came into fashion, and adults basically started dressing kids like smaller versions of themselves.

In the '70s, unisex fashion, once again, became all the rage.

Then the mid-'80s happened, when gender norms—once again—took over, and pink for girls and blue for boys became basically mandatory.

And it wasn't just clothes. In the '80s, the toy aisle also became strictly divided into boys and girls, trucks and dolls. And, that's when the same thing happened to video games.

Early video games like Pong were totally unisex. In fact, they were marketed to the entire family. *Source: Lien, Tracey. "No Girls Allowed: Unraveling the story behind the stereotype of video games being for boys." Polygon. Vox Media, 02 Dec. 2013. Web.*

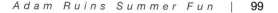

Yes, there's Pac-Man who, as his hecking name implies, was a dude. But the game was so popular with women that when it came time for a sequel, the developers gave it a female main character, Ms. Pac-Man. *Source: "Electronic Games Magazine." May 1982: n. pag. Internet Archive. Internet Archive. Web.*

Not missus, miss. She was a modern '80s career woman.

And not only was much of the audience female—many of the developers were, too.

Among the stars of early game design were Atari's Carol Shaw, "Centipede" creator, and Donna Bailey, "Centipede" developer. Roberta Williams was an adventure game pioneer and company co-founder, whose "King's Quest" series was a massive hit among gamers of all stripes.

But all of that changed during the video game crash of 1983.

Greedy publishers started flooding the market with shoddy games like *I Want My Mommy*, *Lost Luggage*, and *E.T.*, for the Atari 2600, which has been called one of the worst video game consoles of all time. *Source: Gratzer, Karl, and Dieter Stiefel. History of Insolvency and Bankruptcy from an International Perspective. Huddinge: Södertörns Högskola, 2008. Web.*

Most adults stopped playing games entirely, and the video game market cratered.

So, when it came time to market the original Nintendo entertainment system, Nintendo devised a plan. Instead of selling it in the electronics section, they sold it in the toy aisle. But by then, the toy aisle was completely separated into pink and blue—boy and girl. Nintendo had to choose a side.

They went with boy. And then they marketed to those boys relentlessly.

Other brands, like Sega, soon followed suit.

And they kept marketing to those boys as they grew up.

After decades of this kind of advertising, we now think of video games as being the exclusive domain of the male sex.

In reality, more adult women play video games than teenage boys do. *Source: "Essential Facts about the Computer and Videogame Industry." Entertainment Software Association (2015): n. pag. Entertainment Software Association, Apr. 2015. Web.*

Yeah, that's including games for your mobile device. But guess what? Games are games.

All that means is that mainstream consoles like PS4 and Xbox One are refusing to serve a huge, untapped market. We're talking millions of women who would love to play more games, but are being pushed away from the hobby by weird, old-fashioned marketing that publishers are sticking with—seemingly out of sheer force of habit.

Video games are the greatest new art form of the century. They can do anything. Saying they're for just one gender is ridiculous.

When we think about video games in such a limited way, it makes the games worse.

When Nintendo learned that making games just for boys was limiting their audience, they hired a female director to create *Animal Crossing: New Leaf*. The game broke sales records, and 56 percent of the people playing it are women. *Source: Hudson, Laura. "Nintendo's New Key to Creativity: More Women." Wired. Conde Nast, 28 Mar. 2014. Web.*

And with the rise of indie games, more and more female developers are getting to make whole new types of video games.

VOICE OF **KELLEE SANTIAGO**
Co-Founder
thatgamecompany

KELLEE SANTIAGO,

Co-founder of thatgamecompany and
one of the creators of *Journey*:

Kellee Santiago: "When we created *Journey*, we wanted to make a game that anyone could relate to, so our theory was that console video games and gamers were being unfairly pigeonholed into only a limited range of genres. Our goal at *Journey* was to show that games could be about something else, and that both avid and first-time gamers would embrace these new types of games.

"And now developers are really experimenting with reaching all types of players. It's an incredibly exciting time in video games."

IT AIN'T "GAME OVER"

Video games are all about unbridled imagination, so when we set them free of arbitrary restrictions, they're more fun than ever.

Copyright law is the same way. If we just let the public domain flourish, think of all the awesome new works that would be created.

If we looked at our educational system with fresh eyes, we could make sure that every kid has fun summer breaks without the summer slide.

We don't have to keep doing things the same way just because that's how people did them in the past. We have the power to learn about the world and improve it, so that future generations can have fun without limits.

EPISODE TEN

ADAM RUINS
SEX

DIRECTOR: PAUL BRIGANTI
ORIGINAL AIR DATE: DECEMBER 8, 2015

Ooh! How titillating. Sex! *Sexy* sex. In many ways, it's one of the most important things people engage in. It's both a method of procreation and it's really fun. How could it possibly be ruined?

Well....

CREEPY ANTI-MASTURBATION PRUDES POPULARIZED CIRCUMCISION

If you're a dude who isn't Muslim or Jewish and you're circumcised, guess what? That's kind of weird. America is one of the only countries in the world that practices routine non-religious circumcision. *Source: Weiss et al. Male circumcision: global trends and determinants of prevalence, safety and acceptability. WHO, 2007. Web.*

Yet, most of us don't even know why we do it.

By the time your tip got snipped, circumcision had been a tradition for generations.

Chances are, when you popped out, the doctor asked your dad if they wanted you to be circumcised. And your dad did the equivalent of shrugging and saying, "Um, yeah, I guess. I mean, his should look like mine, right?" Much like his dad did...much like his dad's dad did. And so on.

The source of that tradition is real weird.

Mostly, it was done to keep boys from having solo fun with their noodles.

Though religious circumcision had been practiced in the Middle East for a millennia, no one did it in the U.S. until the puritanical nineteenth century, when sex-phobic doctors promoted it as a way of preventing your kids from committing their favorite sin: masturbation. *Source: Gollaher, David. Circumcision: A History of the World's Most Controversial Surgery. Basic Books, 2000.*

One prominent advocate of dingle docking was, and we're not making this up, John Harvey Kellogg, the inventor of cornflakes. *Source: Kellogg, John Harvey. Plain Facts for Old and Young. New York: Arno, 1974. Print.*

Victorian prudes like Kellogg just straight up hated sex and thought that by pruning dudes' peters, they could contain your base and lustful instincts. *Source: Kellogg, John Harvey. Plain Facts for Old and Young. New York: Arno, 1974. Print.*

And you don't even know what he thought you should do to women—things like applying carbolic acid to the clitoris.

But as for dudes and their dangly bits, as everyone is aware, circumcision sure as hell doesn't prevent men from masturbating.

It doesn't keep wieners cleaner, either. That's just another old Victorian myth. These guys had a lot of weird ideas about circumcision. It can help prevent a few rare infections, but so does, you know, washing your dingus. *Source: Singh-Grewal, D., J. Macdessi, and J. Craig. "Circumcision for the Prevention of Urinary Tract Infection in Boys: A Systematic Review of Randomised Trials and Observational Studies." Archives of Disease in Childhood 90 (2004): 853-58. Web.*

Why would you have to cut off part of your body to keep it clean? You don't have to cut off your butt cheeks to keep your butt clean.

YOUR FRIEND THE FORESKIN

The foreskin isn't useless.

The foreskin plays a very important role in sex. It's filled with nerve endings, it protects the glands so it doesn't become desensitized, and it's a natural lubricant—like a hot dog in a buttered bun. *Source: Fleiss, PM, FM Hodges, and RS Van Howe. "Immunological functions of the human pre-puce." Sexually Transmitted Infections. March 1998. Source: United States. National Institute of Health. Male Circumcision Decreases Penile Sensitivity as Measured in a Large Cohort. By Guy Bronselaer, Justine Schober, Heino Meyer-Bahlburg, Guy T'Sjoen, Robert Vlietinck, and Piet Hoebeke. 5th ed. Vol. 111. N.p.: BJU International, 2013. Web.*

Now, circumcision has been found to reduce the rate of HIV acquisition in men by up to 60 percent. *Source: "Male circumcision for HIV prevention." World Health Organization. 2015. Web.*

But condoms reduce it by 80 percent, and they don't require you to uh, you know, cut your dong off. *Source: Weller SC, Davis-Beaty K. "Condom effectiveness in reducing heterosexual HIV transmission." Cochrane Database of Systematic Reviews 2007, Issue 4.*

Circumcision doesn't make your frank and beans "look better" to women, either.

According to anecdotal evidence, women think all wangs look weird. If you like being circumcised, or you did it for religious reasons...fine. There's no harm in it. But as far as we can tell, there's also no particularly compelling reason to do it. And the only reason you were circumcised is because a bunch of nineteenth century prudes were trying to ruin your sex life.

Of course, if we're talking about sex, we gotta talk about STDs. Little buggers like herpes.

But people even have the wrong idea about herpes.

HERPES AIN'T A BIG DEAL

Herpes isn't dangerous. Most of the time it's not even noticeable.

Herpes is generally presented as some nightmare genital disease of Lovecraftian proportions. The CDC even talks about how it'll cause an eruption of red sores. You know, a horrible scarlet letter for everyone's junk. They also say four out of five people who carry it don't know they have it. That it's incurable. That one in six Americans has it. *Source: United States. CDC. Genital Herpes – CDC Fact Sheet (Basic).*

Centers for Disease Control and Prevention, 14 Oct. 2015. Web.

Eruptions of red sores? That's scare mongering. Let's call them what they are: little red bumps. Except, you're already covered with little red bumps. Mosquito bites, ingrown hairs, pimples. To be human is to be covered in little red bumps, yo.

Secondly, the reason four out of five carriers don't know they have it is because they either have no symptoms, or their symptoms are so mild they never notice. *Source: "Herpes Simplex Virus." World Health Organization. World Health Organization, Jan. 2015. Web. 01 Oct. 2015.*

And nearly everyone has it. If you include oral herpes, worldwide, nearly 90 percent of the global population carries some strain of herpes. *Source: Anna Wald and Lawrence Corey. Human Herpesviruses: Biology, Therapy, and Immunoprophylaxis. 2007.*

Let's call in the expert!

DR. JENNIFER LANG,

Board-Certified OB/GYN and Medical Director:

"Some people might have a mild rash around the mouth or genital region, maybe some red or white bumps. The truth is, if you're not immuno-compromised or in the late stages of pregnancy, you really don't have to worry about it. Most sexually active adults are gonna be exposed to herpes at some point in their life. It's really not a big deal. That's what I tell my patients."

The fact is, our culture's fear of herpes is totally out of proportion with how mild the disease actually is. We're treating what's basically junk acne like it's some kind of sexual plague. And that fear is pretty recent. Up until a few decades ago, no one gave a crap about herpes.

But all of that changed in the early '80s. In the hangover from the sexual revolution there was a straight-up cultural freak out about STDs. And even benign diseases, like herpes, got swept up in the puritanical panic.

It made the cover of *Time* in 1982. *Source: Leo, John. "The New Scarlet Letter." Time. Time Inc., 02 Aug. 1982. Web.*

The only serious side effect of herpes is shame. One study found that people consider herpes more shameful than any STD, other than HIV. *Source: Hitti, Miranda. "Genital Herpes: Stigma Still Strong." CBS News. CBS. New York, New York, n.d. CBS News. Web.*

That's crazy. And herpes is so stigmatized that there are multiple online dating sites just for people with herpes. All of this over a disease that 90 percent of people have. You know what else is a herpes dating site? OKCupid, Match.com, and Christian Mingle. All of them—because nine out of ten people have herpes.

The fact that we shame each other this hard over a disease that practically everyone has is truly awful.

Speaking of shame, there's a particular phrase that needs to be eradicated.

KNOCK IT OFF ABOUT "POPPING CHERRIES"

It's not just gross, it's totally wrong. It's not how a hymen works.

People picture the hymen like it's one of those paper banners at a sports game. They think it covers up a lady's vagina, and then when she has sex for the first time, it gets busted.

Everything about that is wrong. OK, think about it. If women's hymens completely sealed their vaginas, where would their periods go? I mean, they'd blow up like the blueberry girl in *Charlie and the Chocolate Factory*.

The hymen is actually a thin stretchy bit around the vagina. In most women, their hymens have an opening that's big enough for tampons, fingers, and yes, getting busy. *Source: Feeney, Nolan. "Living Myths About Virginity." The Atlantic. Atlantic Media Company, 7 Feb. 2014. Web.*

But it's not like a barrier. It's more like a balloon arch.

Still, hymens can break from any number of things. Like doing splits. Or living life.

Even then, hymens can heal. And a lot of them never even get torn in the first place. One study found that 52 percent of sexually active teenage women had intact hymens. *Source: United States. National Institute of Health. Differences in Hymenal Morphology between Adolescent Girls with and without a History of Consensual Sexual Intercourse. By JA Adams, KS Batosh, and N. Kellogg. Archives of Adolescent and Pediatric Medicine, Mar. 2004. Web.*

A hymen, as you probably understand it, is a straight-up myth.

Women's bodies don't come with built-in virginity detectors. And sex isn't "supposed to hurt" the first time. But this horrible idea is everywhere in our culture.

There's a Ska band called Cherry Poppin' Daddies.

Cop shows—you know how much we like those—reinforce it with bad writing, that reinforces the myth that an intact hymen means virgin.

The New York Times got it wrong too when they wrote: "...the hymen, the vaginal membrane that normally breaks in the first act of intercourse..." *Source: Sciolino, Elaine, and Souad Mekhennet. "In Europe, Debate Over Islam and Virginity." The New York Times. The New York Times Company, 10 June 2008. Web.*

AS NOT SEEN ON TV ✂

This episode was one of the first times that the "explaining" role was passed off to a character better equipped than Adam to tell the story—in this case, Emily was a better fit to discuss the hymen than he was. The staff enjoyed mixing it up like this, and later used the convention in other episodes to keep Adam on his toes.

The *Times* knows more about regional politics in Finland than the female body.

And it gets way worse than band names. In some parts of the world, women are forced to show government officials that their hymen is intact. If they don't, they can be denied jobs, barred from making rape accusations, even thrown in jail. *Source: "Indonesia: Military Imposing 'Virginity Tests.'" Human Rights Watch. Human Rights Watch, 13 May 2015. Web.Source: Shafy, Samiha. "'Horribly Humiliating': Egyptian Woman Tells of 'Virginity Tests.'"Spiegel On-line International. Spiegel-Verlag. 10 June, 2011. Web. Source: "AFGHANISTAN: Virginity-related Penalties." IRINnews. IRIN, 26 Apr. 2011. Web.*

Virginity exams are straight up sexual assault. And they don't even prove anything because the hymen doesn't work that way! Physically speaking, virginity doesn't exist. It's just something we made up to be mean to women, like *Entourage*.

SHAME IS THE WORST SEXUAL CONDITION

We're all ashamed. At least a little bit. And that can cause us to treat each other horribly. Like when we humiliate people for having an innocuous disease such as herpes. Or redesign babies' genitals for no reason. Or teach teenage girls that their first sexual experience is gonna be a nightmare.

All of these mistakes were caused by shame. Take the example of Kellogg. He brought in circumcision because masturbation freaked him out. But that's crazy, because we all masturbate.

Masturbation is the safest form of sex, it releases tons of healthy endorphins, and it can actually be used to treat sexual dysfunction.

We need to stop doing this to ourselves. No one needs to worry if they like to flick the bean, if they're a virgin, or if they find learning obscure facts deeply erotic. Shame is ruining our sex lives.

We shouldn't let it any longer.

ADAM RUINS
NUTRITION

DIRECTOR: PAUL BRIGANTI
ORIGINAL AIR DATE: DECEMBER 15, 2015

Do you watch daytime TV? Oh, you do? Jeez, it's awful, ain't it? Ceaseless blathering aside—and that could be about any number of mundane topics—there's also an alarming amount of misinformation. Often, it comes from "doctors" who have "great tips" on everything from upping your happiness levels, to which foods cause cancer, to which foods cure cancer. Well, they're all full of crap.

I'M NOT A DOCTOR BUT
I PLAY ONE ON TV

It's always a younger, accomplished "doctor" with a disarming smile. He's in shape. Charming. Wears his hospital scrubs on the stage in front of the studio audience to project some air of "on the job"-ness. But really, he looks more like he's going to a photo shoot than performing any kind of life-saving operation.

AND THEY GIVE TERRIBLE ADVICE

The quacks who've taken over daytime TV often say things like: "Vitamins are the key to health, perhaps the cure for the common cold." Then they'll say something about mega doses, where you ingest *a ton* of a given vitamin.

Here's the thing.

Vitamin supplements don't cure colds, they don't prolong your life, and in some cases, they may actually be harmful.

Vitamins are a collection of various micronutrients that are essential for your body to function normally. By definition vitamins are nutrients we only need a tiny little bit of. *Source: "Vitamin." Merriam-Webster. Merriam-Webster Incorporated, 2015. Web.*

And normally, we get plenty of them from the food we eat.

But what, you ask yourself in a panic, if you get scurvy?

You won't.

Scurvy is caused by an extreme lack of vitamin C. Pirates used to get it because they ate nothing but hard-tack biscuits for months. But if you eat normal food in normal quantities, you'll be fine. Like, just eat a lemon...ever.

TOO MUCH OF SOMETHING ISN'T GOOD

Vitamins are sorta like cats. If you have no cats, you'll be lonely. If you have a cat or two, you'll feel better. But that's enough cats. No one needs to load up on cats. And just like with cats, you don't want to overdo it. Studies show that taking too much of some vitamins, like A, D, or E, can actually make you sick.

And mega doses cure exactly this: nothing.

Vitamin C does not treat or cure the common cold, and products that claim it does are nonsense.

Remember Airborne?

Airborne is a cocktail of plain old vitamins that was marketed as a "cure for the common cold." But in 2006, they were sued for false advertising and ended up paying out 23 million dollars. *Source: Nizza, Mike. "Makers of Airborne Settle False-Ad Suit With Refunds." The New York Times. The New York Times Company, 04 Mar. 2008. Web.*

Airborne hasn't been shown to cure anything. It's basically just bubbles.

At least fifteen different studies have concluded that vitamin C does not treat the common cold. *Source: Offit, Paul. "The Vitamin Myth: Why We Think We Need Supplements." The Atlantic. Atlantic Media Company, 19 July 2013. Web.*

THIS IS
LINUS PAULING'S FAULT

Linus Pauling was a genius chemist, and the only person in history to be awarded two solo Nobel Prizes. He was one of America's true scientific celebrities.

In the early '70s, Paul became obsessed with the idea of living forever and basically went vitamin crazy.

He began claiming that massive doses of vitamin C could prevent the common cold, prolong your life, and even cure cancer. And because he was a celebrity scientist, the media trusted him.

But repeated studies have proven that Pauling was totally wrong. There is no medical basis for his claims. And in 1994, he actually died of cancer, the very disease he claimed vitamins would cure. *Source: Offit, Paul. "The Vitamin Myth: Why We Think We Need Supplements." The Atlantic. Atlantic Media Company, 19 July 2013. Web.*

In a nutshell: Vitamin supplements are a lie, and we only believe in them because one man went crazy.

Pauling was the Michael Jackson of nutrition. He totally changed the game. We had no idea how crazy he was, and forty years later, we're still humming the tunes.

That doesn't mean you shouldn't listen to the experts. You just need to remember that experts can be wrong too. You still need to critically examine ideas, even when they come from a certifiable genius. Or a very handsome TV show host.

Even the conventional wisdom surrounding the "most important meal of the day" is wrong.

Yeah, it's true.

EVERYTHING YOU KNOW ABOUT BREAKFAST IS WRONG

Let's start with OJ. Juice commercials would have you believe that every sip comes right from the tree.

Even orange juice not from concentrate is just as processed as any other mass market food.

Orange juice has an extremely short shelf life, so to stop it from spoiling, manufacturers extract all the oxygen from the juice. *Source: Hamilton, Alissa. "Freshly Squeezed: The Truth About Orange Juice in Boxes." Civil Eats, 06 May 2009. Web.*

But that process also removes all the orange flavor. So manufacturers artificially jam it back in by using flavor packs. *Source: Hamilton, Alissa. "Freshly Squeezed: The Truth About Orange Juice in Boxes." Civil Eats, 06 May 2009. Web.*

It ain't natural.

The taste that you know as Tropicana, Florida's Natural, or Minute Maid, was actually designed in the same lab that makes perfume for Calvin Klein and Dior. The trick is, since the flavor packs are technically made of orange byproducts, they don't have to write "artificially flavored" on the label. But they are.

But flavor packs aren't bad for you.

What's bad for you about orange juice is the sugar.

OJ is loaded with it. An eight-ounce glass of Tropicana contains twenty-two grams of sugar. *Source: "100% Pure Squeezed Sunshine." Tropicana. Tropicana Products, Inc., n.d. Web.*

That's almost as much as a Pepsi, which makes sense since Tropicana is owned by Pepsi. *Source: "The Facts About Your Favorite Beverages." Pepsico. PepsiCo Inc., n.d. Web.*

MILK IS A WHITE LIE, TOO

Remember those "PSAs" they ran in the '90s about how milk did a body good, and made you grow up to be strong?

They were crap. Just for-profit marketing, paid for by the dairy industry.

We've been fed claims like these ever since we were kids. But none of them are true. Repeated research has shown that milk does not help you build strong bones. In fact, one study found that people who drink a lot of milk are at a higher rate of bone fracture. *Source: Carroll, Aaron E. "Got Milk? Might Not Be Doing You Much Good." The New York Times. The New York Times Company, 17 Nov. 2014. Web.*

And you don't need milk for calcium.

ALISSA HAMILTON,
Journalist, Author of *Got Milked?*:

"You know, there's calcium everywhere. Gram for gram, most dried herbs have more calcium than milk. Milk is not the wonder food that we once thought it was. A glass of plain milk has thirteen grams of naturally occurring sugar."

We've been told our entire lives that milk is some kind of nutritional necessity, but it's not. It's just another product being marketed like any other. You don't need it.

In fact, while we're at it....

LET'S DITCH CEREAL, TOO

Fun fact: Cereal was invented by sex-hating religious zealots.

Breakfast cereal as we know it was invented by a man named John Harvey Kellogg. Remember the sex chapter? Yeah. He was a real weirdo.

A choice quote from Kellogg: "Masturbation causes insanity. And circumcision is the cure. *Source: Kellogg, John Harvey. Plain Facts for Old and Young. New York: Arno, 1974. Print.*

"The other cure, a delicious bowl of Dr. Kellogg's granola. It preserves your sperm for strength."

Kellogg was following the teachings of an evangelical minister named Sylvester Graham, who believed that sugar and spice were tools of Satan. *Source: Braun, Adee. "Looking to Quell Sexual Urges? Consider the Graham Cracker." The Atlantic. Atlantic Media Company, 15 Jan. 2014. Web.*

Graham was pretty nutty.

He believed in nonsense—like that spicy, rich foods led to impure thoughts and sinful deeds. That they inspired thoughts of sex and the devil.

The original foods these guys invented or inspired were practically inedible. And that was the point.

But despite their weird ideas, Kellogg's cereal and graham crackers were actually a lot healthier than what most people ate back then. But a century later, we filled them both with sugar.

If you gave a bowl of today's cereal to Kellogg or Graham, they would be horrified.

Just forget all of this marketing and think outside the cereal box.

BUT MEDICAL SHOWS ARE THE WORST

They tell you big, fat lies.

Just because you have a TV show doesn't mean you can't be wrong. Heck, both the show and this book are fact-checked, and they could both be wrong.

JOHN BOHANNON,

Reporter, *Science* magazine:

John Bohannon: "I purposefully did a fraudulent study about the health benefits of chocolate, and I convinced the media that eating chocolate helps you lose weight." *Source: Cohen, Paula. "How the 'Chocolate Diet' Hoax Fooled Millions." CBS News. CBS. New York, NY, 29 May 2015. Web.*

Why would he do that?

John Bohannon: "Because nutrition science is totally broken, and I wanted to show that it's actually very easy to fool the media into making those big headlines that cause those crazy diet fads in the first place."

JOHN'S RECIPE FOR COOKING UP A FRAUDULENT STUDY

First you have to take a really skewed sample, rather than a properly balance one.

Next, you need to cherry-pick your data, taking the stuff that supports what you're interested in, and throwing out the rest.

Third, you need to get it published in a shady journal with no academic standards. But it has to have a science-y name like the *International Archives of Medicine*. What's great about journals like that is they'll take any garbage you give them.

Wait, you must be thinking, *don't the science journals have to make sure that the papers are actually, like, scientific?*

John Bohannon: "Well, for most journals, yes. But there are journals that are just out to make a buck, and they'll publish anything you send them. As long as you pay up."

Before this episode aired, we did get a paper published. Look at how beautiful this is: It's called "The Possible Irritating Effects of Nutritional Facts," and it was published in *Advances in Nutrition and Food Technology*.

Know what's in it? Nothing.

It's just the script. It's not even a scientific paper. But because we paid the journal 369 dollars, they published it verbatim, and now we can cite it like any other source.

Anyway! On to John's last step:

You need to put out a press release with exaggerated language to tantalize journalists.

Voilà! You've got a piping hot pan of garbage.

John Bohannon: "Reporters are hungry for content, and they're more than willing to gobble up even faulty science. And in the case of my study, which I have totally unfounded claims, they covered it all over the world."

This pattern is repeated in the media every day. Press-hungry researchers get bad science published in disreputable journals, and medical shows peddle it to the people. But the fact is, most of the nutrition science reported on in the media isn't science at all.

Shows like these give medical advice, mislead people, and convince them of dangerous pseudo-science, just to sell ads. That's not just being a bad doctor—that's being a bad person.

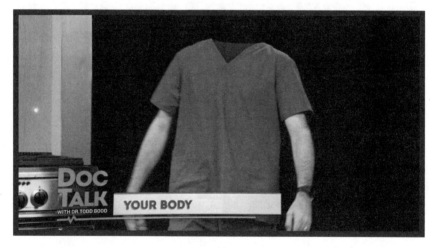

FUN FACT

SKECHERS SHAPE-UP SHOES ARE HOT GARBAGE. SKECHERS WAS ACTUALLY HIT WITH A CLASS ACTION LAWSUIT OVER THEM. THEY ENDED UP SHELLING OUT OVER 40 MILLION DOLLARS.

BUT WE'VE GOT ANSWERS!

Instead of listening to the TV or advertisers, listen to your doctor...your real doctor.

Beyond listening to your doctor, each of us already has the best tool available for tracking health: our bodies.

A great first step in being healthy is to listen to your body. When you eat something bad, you'll know because you'll feel bad. When you eat something good and exercise, you'll feel good. All you have to do is pay attention to what your body says.

Look, you don't have to eat perfectly. Lord knows most of us don't. Just eat in moderation, eat healthy food whenever you can, and get some exercise. That's all you need.

EPISODE TWELVE

ADAM RUINS
DEATH

DIRECTOR: PAUL BRIGANTI
ORIGINAL AIR DATE: DECEMBER 22, 2015

Here's a challenge. Believe what we're about to tell you. Not just hear it, not just understand it, but believe it. It's a fact that you already know to be true, but have never been able to fully accept. And it's this: You are going to die.

You, the person reading right now, are going to die. It's difficult to even to imagine, isn't it? Take a moment and try to picture what it's like to not exist.

You can't do it.

You're imagining darkness, black. But there will be no black. There will be no color, because there will be no you to perceive it.

And your mind recoils from that idea.

It's simply unable to conceive of its own non-existence.

And so, it concludes that it's impossible...that you'll live forever. But you won't. All things end, all motion slow, all heat becomes cold. Life is an eddy in that current of entropy. A brief, chemical reaction that lights up the darkness, and then its fuel spent, dissipates back to nothing. Just like you will. Your body is a marvelous and intricate machine built out of millions of inter-connected fragile systems.

And as you age, each begins to slowly—but surely—deteriorate and break down. When one fails, a doctor may be able to repair it. But at some point, there will be too many interlocking failures to proceed, and like a cascade of dominoes, your joints, your eyes, your heart, your lungs, your memory—your entire body will fail.

It will happen.

And while it's difficult to hear this truth, it is essential that you accept it, because every second that goes by in which you don't is a second of your precious and finite life that you risk wasting. So, I'm going to say it once more, and this time, try as hard as you can to believe me. You, yes you, will die. And there is nothing you can do to stop it.

Yeah. This one is kind of a bummer.

Sorry.

(Not sorry.)

DEATH IS INEVITABLE

It's really important that people accept the above.

Death is inevitable.

The idea of living forever, or of magically being cured of whatever is harming them, is a completely fantasy. People have been trying to "cure death" for millennia. And it's never worked.

In 210 BC, the first emperor of China dosed himself with what he thought were "immortality pills." *Source: Moskowitz, Clara. "The Secret Tomb of China's 1st Emperor: Will We Ever See Inside?" LiveScience. TechMedia Network, 17 Aug. 2012. Web.*

They were mercury pills. He died real fast.

And in the ninth century, an alchemist who was trying to brew an immortality potion made a wee bit of an error. *Source: Rosado, Eric. "The Deadly Irony of Gunpowder." Video blog post. TED Ed. TED Conferences LLC, n.d. Web.*

He actually invented gunpowder. Thanks to his quest for eternal life, millions have been shot dead.

WE'RE NOT ANY CLOSER TO IMMORTALITY NOW

What about cryonics: The idea that you can freeze your body, so it can be revived later?

Eh.

That's medically doubtful. And it assumes that the company that freezes you is going to be around that long. In one famous case, the Cryonics Society of California ran out of money and couldn't keep their customers frozen. *Source: Glass, Ira, and Sam Shaw. "Mistakes Were Made." This American Life. WBEZ. Chicago, Illinois, 18 Apr. 2008. This American Life. Web.*

The bodies began to thaw and decompose.

Then some of the bodies went missing. And to this day, their families still don't know where they went.

Futurists aren't helping things when they suggest garbage like uploading our consciences to hard drives, or the cloud, or whatever. It's ridiculous.

First of all, your brain is a physical organ. That's like saying you could upload your liver onto a computer. And secondly, even if you could, your consciousness wouldn't teleport onto the computer. You would just have created a pretty accurate AI simulation of yourself.

We've never been able to stop death, and we never will.

Which makes the funeral industry all the more horrifying and insidious.

CAPITALIZING ON GRIEF

Sure, people use funerals to grieve. Won't hold that against anyone. But that's one of the reasons it's so gross that the American funeral industry exploits death.

Case in point: The expensive and useless process of embalming, which was popularized during the Civil War.

After Abraham Lincoln was assassinated, the government paraded his corpse around the country in order to showcase the hero's sacrifice. *Source: Fox, Richard Wightman. "A Body for the Body Politic." Slate. The Slate Group. 12 Feb. 2015. Web.*

 But that's not what the people took away from it.

For those of us whose bodies aren't going on tour, embalming is totally pointless. Why would you need to be preserved right before you're buried in the dirt? Isn't the whole point to decompose?

Embalming is the least respectful thing you can do to a body. First, the jaw is wired shut and the eyes are sealed with glue. Then the internal organs are punctured and drained through a hole in the abdomen. After that, they pump the arteries full of formaldehyde... and stuff the internal cavities full of cotton. *Source: Ortner, Pamela, MS, RN, CHPN, and Jeremy Semrau, Ph.D. Exploring Occupational and Environmental Impacts of Conventional vs. "Greener" Funerals and Burials. University of Michigan, 4 Oct. 2012. Web.*

The entire process is a pointless waste of time. Even though funeral directors tell their vulnerable, grieving customers, that embalming is necessary if you want an open casket—and that it keeps the body safe and sanitary—none of it is true. Refrigeration is cheaper, and just as effective, as embalming. *Source: "Embalming Facts." Funeral Consumer Alliance Southern California, n.d. Web.*

And the World Health Organization states that dead bodies pose nearly no health risks to the living. *Source: "Risks posed by dead bodies after disasters." World Health Organization. 2010. Web.*

It's completely safe to touch them.

Which is ironic, because formaldehyde isn't safe. It's a carcinogen. *Source: "Formaldehyde: What expert agencies say." American Cancer Society, n.d. Web.*

SO WHY DO WE STILL DO THIS?

Simple: Money.

Sure hope you enjoy caskets. It's one of the most expensive things you'll ever buy.

Funeral homes can charge upwards of 10,000 dollars for a coffin.

To make things worse, your local funeral home might not be all that local.

A lot of "local" funeral homes are owned by a mega-corporation named SCI, which buys up mom-and-pop shops, but keeps the old name so no one notices. *Source: Barrett, Paul M. "Is Funeral Home Chain SCI's Growth Coming at the Expense of Mourners?" Bloomberg Business. Bloomberg L.P., 24 Oct. 2013. Web.*

They really are a cash cow.

WHAT'S THE ALTERNATIVE?

You could choose cremation.

But there's also natural burial.

CAITLIN DOUGHTY,

Licensed Mortician, Advocate for Natural Burial, Owner of Undertaking LA Funeral Home:

"In natural burial, we dig a hole in the ground and place the body in, in just a shroud. No chemical embalming, no heavy metal casket, no concrete-lined vault.

"It's completely safe. Humans have been burying their bodies like this for tens of thousands of years. But when the funeral industry started, it really took the power away from the grieving families.

"I think that my job as a mortician should just be to facilitate you taking the power around the time of death. You can be involved as much or as little as you want to be. But it can be really intimate and beautiful way to say goodbye to someone you love."

If this is something you want, that's beautiful, and we encourage you to do so.

But unless you plan ahead....

EVERYTHING ABOUT YOUR DEATH WILL SUCK

Death is hard.

That's why it's so important that you accept that one day you will grow old and die. If you don't, you'll end up making terrible medical decisions.

Allow room for conversation.

Here's a dramatized conversation right here!

BERNARD "BUD" HAMMES, PHD
Director of Respecting Choices
GUNDERSEN HEALTH SYSTEM

DR. BUD HAMMES,
Director of Respecting Choices for Gundersen Health System:

Dr. Hammes: "I'm glad you guys are here. I have a story to tell you."

Adam: "Oh, this is my favorite book. It's about how I get prostate cancer and die. You know, one in seven American men gets prostate cancer...."

Emily: "Prostate cancer, I know, you tell me every time we hang out. Did you write a book about your own death?"

Adam: "It helps make the point. Would you read it to us, Bud?"

Dr. Hammes: "I'd be delighted to read it to you. So, here's the problem. Patients and their doctors most often don't have conversations about when the burdens of treatment would be so high, they wouldn't outweigh the benefits of the treatment."

Adam: "If you can't face having an honest conversation about death with your doctor, you can end up chasing unnecessary treatments that do very little to prolong your life and just make your final days really uncomfortable." *Source: Gawande, Atul. Being Mortal. New York: Henry Holt and Company, 2014. Print.*

Dr. Hammes: "Now's the time to make these plans for future healthcare decisions. It's a time to talk with your family about your values, your preferences and your goals, so they don't end up guessing when they make your decisions."

Emily: "I mean, I wouldn't mind that. Murph, my fiancé, he would know what I want."

Dr. Hammes: "That's an understandable point of view, a lot of people think that. But the research is very clear. When families don't have these conversations, the family members are no better than strangers at making these decisions. They end up guessing."

Adam: "And that can be really, really hard on them."

Dr. Hammes: "Sometimes the conflicts are so severe, I don't know that the family will ever talk to each other again."

Emily: "But, it's such a hard conversation to have. I mean, I don't, I don't know where I would begin."

Dr. Hammes: "So, Emily, there are three simple questions everyone should consider. The first is: If you couldn't make your own decisions, who would make decisions on your behalf?

"The second is: If you suffered a serious and permanent brain injury, how bad would it have to be for you to change your goals of care?"

Emily: "Well, I wouldn't want to be kept alive if I was brain dead. Which I guess right now I might be."

Dr. Hammes: "The third question is, do you have any strong-held values or beliefs that would influence how medical decisions might be made?"

Emily: "Um...I don't know. Honestly, these are really tough questions to field right now."

Dr. Hammes: "Well, you're right, Emily. They are hard to answer. That's why in La Crosse, Wisconsin, we decided to approach all of our patients and offer them the opportunity to do this plan. That way, families have the confidence that they made the right decisions."

AS NOT SEEN ON TV ✂

Head writer Travis Helwig ended this episode with the death of Hayley, Adam's love interest throughout the first half of Season One. But everyone on staff enjoyed working with actress Hayley Marie Norman so much that they spent months ribbing Travis for killing off one of their favorite characters.

Death will always be a terrible loss. But if you can accept its inevitability, it makes the whole process a lot easier.

That said....

DEATH IS F*#&ING SCARY AND IT'S ALL RIGHT TO BE AFRAID

Nothing you can learn about death or the way people are taken advantage of by the funeral industry makes death any less terrifying.

It's OK not to know.

It's OK to be sad.

It's OK to be lost.

Death is just a part of life.

ADAM RUINS
HOLLYWOOD

DIRECTOR: TIM WILKIME
ORIGINAL AIR DATE: AUGUST 23, 2016

As you can probably guess, the place they call La-La Land is lousy with La-La Lies. From the glitzy red carpet, to behind the scenes at the biggest awards, to the sets of not-so-real reality shows, it's all garbage. And Adam is here to learn ya something.

THE RED CARPET IS ONE BIG AD

We idolize celebrities for their style and fashion, but the truth is, everything from their jewelry to their shoes is marketing—picked out by brands looking to make a buck.

RACHEL BLOOM,

Co-creator/Star, *Crazy Ex-Girlfriend:*

Rachel Bloom: "Celebrities don't wake up looking stunning. They have people to prepare them."

[This is how normal humans can look when waking up.]

Rachel Bloom: "Most of the time we look schlubbier than the crowd at a Dave Matthews concert. But anybody would look fantastic if they had a pit crew of hair and makeup experts Frankensteining them for six hours."

They don't even pick their clothes. Their pit crew does.

[The team.]

Rachel Bloom: "My stylist tells me what to wear, and then the designers' marketing team says yes or no, depending on whether or not they think I'll sell the product. Sometimes the designer can refuse to loan somebody a dress if that person doesn't fit their brand, or has the wrong body type...I'm basically a human NASCAR."

It's not style. It's not fashion.

It's advertising.

When Mark McGrath asks, "Who are you wearing?" all of America will hear that brand's name.

AS NOT SEEN ON TV ✂

The idea for Rachel Bloom's red carpet bit came from Bloom herself, who knows Adam and several staffers from their College Humor days.

EVEN THE AWARDS THEMSELVES ARE A LIE

Award shows don't determine the best movie of the year.

Money can't act, but it can make voters act differently. And to influence them, studios and networks throw boatloads of money into what the industry calls "For Your Consideration" campaigns.

"For Your Consideration" campaigns are a very specific form of marketing that's aimed solely at awards voters. They're not quite bribery, but they're close.

Voters get free movies. Gifts. They throw lavish parties for voters to meet celebrities. *Source: Fox, Jesse David. "A Brief History of Harvey Weinstein's Oscar Campaign Tactics." Vulture. New York Media, LLC, 29 Jan. 2014. Web.*

Not to mention the ads the studios plaster all over LA.

The worst offenders are the Golden Globes. Only the eighty-seven members of the Hollywood Foreign Press get to vote, and since everyone in Hollywood knows who they are, they get campaigned to personally.

One year, Sharon Stone's people sent the members gold, Coach watches. So, yeah, she got the nod. *Source: Shone, Tom. "In Praise of the Golden Globes." Slate. Graham Holdings Company, 13 Jan. 2012. Web.*

This process is such an open secret, Denzel Washington joked about it on air during an acceptance speech.

Denzel Washington: "Some of you may know Freddie Fields, he invited me to the first Hollywood Foreign Press luncheon. He said they're gonna watch the movie, we're gonna feed them, they're gonna come over, you're gonna take pictures with everybody, you're gonna hold the magazines, take the pictures, and you're gonna win the award I won that year." *Source: Jang, Meena. "Golden Globes: Denzel Washington Accepts Cecil B. DeMille Award." The Hollywood Reporter. Prometheus Global Media, 10 Jan. 2016. Web.*

And all that advertising costs money. To win an Oscar, studios may have to spend up to ten million dollars. *Source: Buckley, Cara. "Oscars 2016: The Race May Yet Heat Up." New York Times 2 Dec. 2015: C1. Web.*

PETE HAMMOND,

Awards Columnist, *Deadline Hollywood*:

"Look, it's all about the bottom line. There are studies that show a nomination itself can mean 20 million dollars more at the box office, and with a win, it can be 35 million dollars and up. Actually, even a flopped movie can make money with a nomination. *Source: Ryzik, Melena. "The Value of the Oscar Bump." New York Times. The New York Times Company, 26 Jan. 2011. Web.*

"Getting nominated is just good for business.

"Quality can matter, but really, you've got to campaign. Studios do all sorts of things now to get attention from voters: They have concerts, trips to Vegas. Nominees will even come to your house now. Look, spending money doesn't guarantee you're gonna win, but if you wanna have a chance, you'd better campaign."

IT'S ALSO ABOUT PRESTIGE AND POWER

No one was taking Netflix seriously as a TV network. So they resolved to win an Emmy. They went to the neighborhoods of Emmy voters and gave their neighbors 50 dollars each to put up Netflix lawn signs. They sent out food trucks with free lunch all around Los Angeles. They painted the town with money. And that year, they won not only one Emmy, they won three. Now Netflix is a TV network. *Source: Andreeva, Nellie. "Emmys: Netflix Uses Lawn Signs in 'House of Cards,' 'Arrested Development' Campaign." Deadline. PMC, 24 Jun. 2013. Web.*

That doesn't mean the movies and shows you enjoy are secretly horrible. The ones that get nominated are usually pretty good.

But when it comes to who wins, money talks.

EVEN THE *RATINGS* MOVIES GET ARE POINTLESS

Can anyone think of a reason why a sixteen-year-old can't handle an R-rated flick, but a seventeen-year-old can?

Movie ratings are an outdated and unnecessary form of censorship that makes no sense. It all goes back to the uptight and prohibition '20s.

Movies back then were starting to get a little racy, so the government threatened to censor the movie industry—until a man named William Haye stepped in, and created the Hays Code. *Source: The Motion Picture Production Code of 1930. Web.*

The Hays Code eventually evolved into the rating system we have today, and while today's system is a lot less racist, it is just as weird and arbitrary.

Who makes the ratings anyway?

That's the spooky part: No one knows. The identities of the ratings board members are kept secret. All we know is that they're parents who live in Los Angeles. *Source: MPAA, 2016. Web.*

We *do* know that the ratings they give are totally irrational.

What is a teenager excited to see in their first R-rated movie that they can't in PG-13?

Violence? *Lots* of violence? Wrong.

PG-13 movies have been found to contain more gun violence than R-rated movies. *Source: Kang, Cecilia. "The Violent 'Taken' movies are rated PG-13. Do ratings make sense anymore?" Washington Post. Washington Post Company, 20 Oct. 2014. Web.*

In fact, gun violence in PG-13 movies has tripled since 1985. *Source: Bushman, Brad J., et al. "Gun violence trends in movies." Pediatrics 132.6 (2013): 1014-1018.*

Thanks, MPAA.

What you won't get in PG-13 flicks is sex.

For a group that's totally chill about hyper-violent blood symphonies, the MPAA is weirdly prudish about sex. They gave a PG-13 rating to *The Dark Knight*, a movie where dozens are brutally murdered, a hospital explodes, and a bomb is planted in a dude's belly.

And an R rating to *Shakespearean Love*, an Oscar winning, literary dramedy with some mild hanky panky.

The MPAA straight-up loves violence and hates sex, and no one knows why.

Even swearing isn't immune to the nonsense. The MPAA often gives different ratings to the very same word. *Source: "This Film is Not Yet Rated," 2006. Film.*

To wit:

If a woman says, "[BLEEP] you," to a guy, it'll be PG-13.

If a woman says, "I want to [BLEEP] you," it'll get an R.

If a man says, "I'd like to [BLEEP] you," to another man, that's NC-17—because they routinely rate LGBT sex as more objectionable than straight sex. *Source: Child, Ben. "US censors accused of homophobia over restrictive Pride rating." The Guardian. Guardian Media Group, 2 Oct. 2014. Web.*

How do they justify it?

They don't.

Joan Graves, the Chair of the MPAA Ratings Board: "It's not science, it's a matter of perception." *Source: Sneed, Tierney. "Don't Expect Any Major Changes to the MPAA Ratings System in 2014." U.S. News & World Report. U.S. News & World Report, L.P., 7 Jan. 2014. Web.*

This means they can use whatever weird logic or prejudice they want.

Yeah. It sucks and it makes no sense.

In principle, it's important to know what kids are watching. But the system we currently have is outdated, arbitrary, and kind of homophobic. It helps no one.

AND REALITY SHOWS DON'T HAVE SQUAT TO DO WITH REALITY

It's all fake! Fake fake fake!

So, what the heck is going on?

MIKE KOPPLIN,

Reality Show Producer, *Bridezillas,*
***Hardcore Pawn: Chicago*:**

Mike Kopplin: "Most people know that reality shows bend the truth, but they don't understand how staged they really are."

Reality shows have "story producers" (a.k.a., writers) and scripts.

Some reality shows are so scripted, they've actually been unionized by the Writers Guild of America. *Source: "Reality & Game Show Writers." Writers Guild of America. Web.*

Mike Kopplin: "Now, every show is different, but they all start with a basic level of planning, from establishing talking points beforehand to actually doing reshoots. Like on *Bridezillas*, for instance, we would go out and reshoot the bride if she was too nice. We'd have her go crazy and yell and scream and carry on. Now, celebrity shows, they can be *very* scripted."

These are not celebrities "inviting you into their lives."

Think about it.

If the celebrity's entire livelihood is their image, do you really think they're gonna let cameras into their home without some kind of a plan?

Mike Kopplin: "And TV shows are very expensive to make, so we have to prove to the network before the shoot date that we're gonna get usable footage, because a perfect three-act story doesn't just fall into our laps."

And yet, even with the scripts, editing is often used to trim down speech to make it snappier.

These are called "Frankenbites."

KENT KINCANNON,
Editor, *Adam Ruins Everything:*

"A Frankenbite is when editors combine and trim sentences to make them more concise. When you hear somebody say something and it's off screen, it's probably a Frankenbite. You can even use Frankenbites to make people say things they didn't actually say."

Does this mean all your favorite reality shows are fake?

To some extent, yes.

The people on house hunting shows have already bought one of the houses and just removed all the furniture to make it look vacant. Source: Friedman, Marcelle. "Why It Matters That House Hunters Is Fake." Slate. Graham Holdings Company, 14 Jun. 2012. Web.

Food competition shows let contestants recook fresh plates of food. Source: Sietsema, Robert. "Iron Chef Boyardee." Village Voice. Voice Media Group, 19 Feb. 2008. Web.

The Alaskan bush people actually live in Seattle. *Source: Park, Andrea. "Alaskan Bush People Stars Plead Guilty to Lying About Living In Alaska to Collect Oil Revenue Checks." People. Time Inc., 20 Nov. 2015. Web.*

And the producers on *The Bachelor* plan all the dates and tell the bachelor who to send home when. *Source: Fedotowsky, Ali. "Behind-the-Scenes Secrets You Need to Know About the First Rose Ceremony!" E! News. NBC Universal, 7 Jan. 2014. Web.*

Reality shows want you to believe that they're real life, but the truth is, they're as fake as everything else on TV.

And that's all right.

ARIANA MADIX,

Star, *Vanderpump Rules*:

"A lot of Hollywood is an illusion. But as long as they're honest about the extent of that illusion, it's OK. *Vanderpump Rules* is actually really real. We're all really friends, we all get in tons of fights, and I actually do work at the restaurant. But that tough conversation I have to have with my boyfriend, I know where it's gonna take place cause that table is surrounded by cameras and lights. Much like a lot of Hollywood, it's real and it's produced. But that's OK, as long as you know the difference."

Adam Ruins Everything is the same way.

Yes, Adam is a know-it-all in real life too, but there's no way one person could learn all of these facts alone. That's why he has the help of writers and researchers. Heck, half the time he's just reading lines they wrote.

The point is, there's nothing wrong with a little Hollywood magic... as long as everyone knows it's a magic trick. Hopefully, by being up front about how we make our show, we've helped generate a little bit of trust.

ADAM RUINS

FOOTBALL

DIRECTOR: TIM WILKIME
ORIGINAL AIR DATE: AUGUST 30, 2016

In this episode, Adam's big playbook is filled with cold, hard facts. Among them: playoffs almost never determine which team is best, myths about hydration are putting kids at risk, and why the game must change due to football-related brain injuries.

ARE THEY EVEN "YOUR" TEAMS?

Let's get philosophical for a minute here.

Sports fans often consider local, major league teams to be "theirs" in some capacity. Why?

None of the players are from there, they change every year, and "your" team may have just switched cities.

It reminds us of a famous thought experiment.

Imagine a sandwich, and that sandwich is your team. Over time, every part of it changes. The turkey gets traded to Denver, the tomato gets suspended for dog fighting, and the bread can't close a stadium deal. So, a philosopher would ask, is it even the same sandwich?

Everything but the name changes year to year, but we still love our team just as much. It's like we're really just a fan of the logo and we want our logos to win the playoffs.

EXCEPT EVEN THE PLAYOFFS ARE NONSENSE

The playoffs don't pick which team is best. In fact, the playoffs are a random and chaotic system that's little better than a coin toss.

In fact, they more or less pick the winner at random.

Historically, the team with the best record wins the Super Bowl less than half the time. It's actually more common for a worse team to win. *Source: Boeck, Scott. "For Super Bowl winners, the most vital stat to victory is..." USA Today. Gannett Company, 27 Jan. 2009. Web.*

Case in point: the 2011 New York Giants.

They weren't number one, they were number ten.

The Giants' regular season record that year was nine and seven, the worst record of any team to ever win a Super Bowl. But in the playoffs they beat the Packers, who had only lost a single game all year.

Hate to tell you this, but the Giants weren't the better team. They were definitely the worse team, and they just got lucky.

Any team can win one game. The problem with the playoffs is they have way too small of a sample size.

Let's put it in different terms. Let's stack Bruce Springsteen up against Billy Joel.

Over his career, Billy has won six Grammys.

Bruce has won twenty.

But on February 25, 1981, Billy beat Bruce for best rock vocal performance. *Source: "23rd Annual GRAMMY Awards." Grammy.org. Web.*

If you decide the whole contest based on one day in February, Billy wins.

It's exactly the same with the playoffs. Just because you win on one day, it doesn't make you the better team. It's luck.

BASEBALL IS EVEN WORSE

In fact, it's the most random major sport.

Since 1995, the team with the best regular season record has won the World Series just 16 percent of the time. *Source: Terbush, Jon. "May the best team not win: Baseball's winningest clubs rarely win the World Series." The Week. Dennis Publishing, 7 Oct. 2013. Web.*

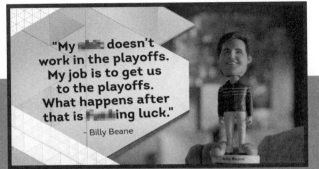

BILLY BEANE,

Legendary Oakland A's General Manager:

"My [BEEP] doesn't work in the playoffs. My job is to get us to the playoffs. What happens after that is [BEEP] luck."

Long story short, might as well skip the Super Bowl and award the championship to whoever wins the coin flip.

But the randomness is why we like the playoffs. That's when the objectively worse underdogs can beat their athletic superiors.

Face it: We don't like sports because they're rational. We like them because they're random and make no sense.

Speaking of not making sense, let's talk sports myths.

EVERYTHING YOU KNOW ABOUT HYDRATION IS WRONG

The risk of dehydration is way overblown.

In America, we've become obsessed with the "dangers" of dehydration. People think that if they're not constantly drinking water, they risk death.

Do you need eight glasses of water a day? No study has ever shown or even claimed that to be true—it's just something people say.

People also say water prevents cramps. But you didn't hear it from science, because science says neither of those claims are true.
Source: McIntosh, James. "Only drink when thirsty to avoid health risks." Medical News Today. MediLexicon International Ltd., 30 Jun. 2015. Web.

Just drink when you're thirsty.

TAMARA HEW-BUTLER DPM, PHD
Exercise Physiologist
OAKLAND UNIVERSITY

TAMARA HEW-BUTLER,
Professor of Exercise Science at Oakland University:

"Our bodies already possess an extremely sensitive measure of dehydration. It's called thirst. As long as we drink when we feel thirst, we really won't dehydrate. That's how humans have done it for millions of years, and it's worked out fine.

"As long as you have free access to water, and you drink when you're thirsty, you'll be fine."

The fact is, truly dangerous levels of dehydration are incredibly rare and only occur in cases of extreme sickness or isolation.

So, why are we so terrified of dehydration?

BLAME ADVERTISING

These companies have consistently portrayed dehydration as a serious threat for one simple reason: it gets us to drink more.

The International Bottled Water Association publishes a hydration calculator that can recommend you drink two liters of water a day. *Source: "Hydration Calculator." International Bottled Water Association. Web.*

Dasani tells you that hydration is healthy. So, drink up—preferably Dasani.

Paid spokesman Dustin Pedroia says he always hydrates with Vita Coco because it prevents cramps...even though there's no proof that it does.

And in *Runner's World Magazine*, Gatorade ran an ad masquerading as an article titled Hydration 101. *Source: Gatorade Sports Science Institute: Hydration 101. Advertisement. Runner's World. June 2002: Print.*

It included tips like, "Drink early and often, don't wait until you feel thirsty, and always drink sports drinks."

Here's where it gets sticky. That ad was sponsored by the Gatorade Sports Science Institute, which was founded by Gatorade in 1985.

Its scientific mission? To discover exciting new reasons people should drink their product. *Source: Eig, Jonathan. "Gatorade's Formula For Staying On Top: A Blitz of Research." Wall Street Journal. News Corp, 5 May 2000. Web.*

Gatorade also sponsors sports science research at universities across America, and this can influence their findings. The American College of Sports Medicine once recommended: "When exercising, you should drink 'as much as tolerable.'" *Source: Convertino, Victor A., et al. "American College of Sports Medicine position stand. Exercise and fluid replacement." Medicine and science in sports and exercise 28.1 (1996): i-vii.*

Other companies soon followed suit. Evian's parent company founded Hydration for Health, a group that "promotes healthy hydration habits by sharing scientific research."

And after decades of bad science and marketing, we now believe dehydration is a dire threat.

If you're thinking, "Well, it's not like drinking too much liquid's gonna kill anybody."

THAT'S EXACTLY WHAT IT CAN DO

All this scare mongering over dehydration has created an entirely different problem: over-hydration.

And you can't just pee out the excess if you're exercising.

Exercise stops you from peeing by putting your body in water conservation mode. And if you over-hydrate then, all that extra fluid has nowhere to go.

It's called Exercise Associated Hyponatremia, and it can be deadly.

In a study of the 2002 Boston Marathon, nearly one-sixth of the runners studied were found to have hyponatremia. These runners drank so much liquid during the race that by the finish line, they had actually gained weight. *Source: Almond, Christopher SD, et al. "Hyponatremia among runners in the Boston Marathon." New England Journal of Medicine 352.15 (2005): 1550-1556.*

This is a serious problem in sports. At least twelve athletes have died from over-hydration. *Source: Winter, George. "Over-drinking can be deadlier than dehydration." The Telegraph. Telegraph Media Group, 26 Mar. 2012. Web.*

TAMARA HEW-BUTLER,

Professor of Exercise Science at Oakland University:

"Over-hydration is dangerous. Most researchers, including myself, think that it's the marketing of the beverage industry that's responsible for this surge in Fluid Overload Hyponatremia."

If you're a coach, or if you assist kids on the field, don't feel bad.

Death by hyponatremia is extremely rare. Just give kids free access to water, let them drink when they're thirsty, and don't treat ads as science.

THAT WHOLE CONCUSSION THING

Everything you know about football and brain injuries is wrong.

The NFL claims to take concussions seriously, but the rate of diagnosed concussions keeps rising—and those are just the ones we know about, since as many as 80 percent are never even reported. *Source: Baugh, Christine M., et al. "Frequency of Head-Impact–Related Outcomes by Position in NCAA Division I Collegiate Football Players." Journal of Neurotrauma 32.5 (2015): 314-326.*

The truth is, our national conversation about brain injuries in football misses the point entirely, because concussions are just the tip of the iceberg.

The brain disorder found in football players is called Chronic Traumatic Encephalopathy, or CTE. And here's the hard truth—it's not just caused by concussion.

It's also caused by the tiny, run-of-the-mill hits that happen dozens of times a game.

These are totally routine tackles and plays that happen over and over again in every game, especially to linemen. But research now shows that even little hits like these cause CTE, which could lead to lifelong memory loss, depression, aggression, dementia, anxiety, and even suicide.

DR. ANN MCKEE,

Professor of Neurology at Boston University, and Director of the CTE Center:

Dr. Ann McKee: "Unfortunately it's true—CTE isn't just caused by concussions, it's also caused by the small subconcussive hits that build up over time. If you play football at any level, the chronic hits to the head will cause brain damage."

Does it happen to everyone?

Dr. Ann McKee: "We found CTE in over 96 percent of former professional players' brains that we've studied. *Source: Breslow, Jason M. "New: 87 Deceased NFL Players Test Positive for Brain Disease." Frontline. PBS, 18 Sep. 2015. Web.*

"The fact is, our research shows that it's practically impossible to play football without suffering irreversible brain damage."

The answer isn't to "build better helmets," either.

When the body and head suddenly stop, the brain stretches, breaking its internal structures. Unless you can fit a helmet inside your skull, there is no way to stop it.

YEAH, THE NFL KNOWS ABOUT IT

In fact, the NFL has admitted that playing football is linked to CTE. They just don't take it seriously. When asked whether football was dangerous, NFL commissioner, Roger Goodell, said: "There's risk in life. There's risk to sitting on the couch." *Source: Gutierrez, Paul. "Roger Goodell: If I had son, I'd 'love' to have him play football." ESPN. ESPN, Inc., 5 Feb. 2016. Web.*

I don't know about you, but if my couch was giving brain damage to 96 percent of the people that sat on it, I would throw out that couch.

But, hey, maybe it's easy to ignore the truth when you're getting paid 34 million dollars a year to maintain the status quo. *Source: Knowlton, Emmett. "The non-profit NFL has paid Roger Goodell nearly $80 million the last 2 years." Business Insider. Axel Springer SE, 16 Feb. 2016. Web.*

AS NOT SEEN ON TV ✂

Mary Lordes, the episode's writer, is a big Philadelphia Eagles fan!

Yeah. NFL players can make their own decisions. They're adults.

But....

KIDS CAN'T

There are less than 2,000 current NFL players, but more than one million high school students play the game, as well as hundreds of thousands of straight-up kids.

Dr. Ann McKee: "Children's brains are especially susceptible to brain damage. The truth is, the brain isn't even finished developing until age 25. It's difficult to say this, but children simply should not be allowed to play football."

Just ask the players if you think that's overboard.

Troy Aikman: "If I had a ten-year-old boy, I don't know that I'd be real inclined to encourage him to go play football." *Source: Aikman, Troy. Real Sports with Bryant Gumbel. HBO. 25 Jan. 2011. Web.*

Mike Ditka: "If you had an eight-year old kid now, would you tell him you wanted him to play football? I wouldn't. My whole life was football."

Harry Carson: "Especially me—knowing what I know now—there's absolutely no way, no way in hell, that I would do it all over again."

Source: Carson, Harry. Frontline. PBS, 4 Sep. 2013. Web.

Look, it's hard to hear that the game we love is killing people and hurting kids. But it's true.

THERE'S A WAY
TO FIX THIS

If we keep playing football the same old way, players will keep dying, parents will pull the next generation of athletes out of the sport, and the game we love will slowly fade from prominence... just like boxing and horseracing did. *Source: Nelson, Murry R. American Sports: A History of Icons, Idols, and Ideas. Westport: Greenwood, 2013. Print.*

Tastes do change. But they don't have to. We can save football by changing it.

Eliminating tackling and getting rid of linemen would do the trick.

But maybe you'd think it wouldn't be football anymore.

That's what they thought back in 1905. Then, the sport was so violent that college players were getting trampled to death. There were eighteen deaths nationwide that year alone.

Teddy Roosevelt insisted that football should legalize the forward pass, making the game safer by opening up the field. That made the game fundamentally different forever—but it was still football.

We have a choice. We either do the hard thing and make real changes to the game, or we keep ignoring the problem and fifty years from now, football will be dead. And that would be a shame... because football is awesome.

The obvious joke here is that "wedded bliss" is often anything but. However, there's a much more insidious side to the industry and its place in society. This is a process that eats couples' money. Beyond cash, it turns out that soulmates are statistically impossible. And even more interesting, divorce is actually good for society.

IT'S NOT ABOUT TRADITION

It's about money.

Nearly all wedding traditions are nothing but pointless and expensive displays of wealth. In fact, this entire ceremony has been hijacked by a greedy industry looking to make a buck.

AS NOT SEEN ON TV ✂

Working on this episode illustrated just how important it is to have an even gender split in writers' rooms. While pitching ideas and discussing the episode's narrative arc, the team realized just how differently men and women absorb clichés and messaging about romance, dating, and marriage, and how important it was to speak to both. Several of the staff members involved in developing the episode have gotten engaged or married since. Hopefully they're better off after their exposure to scholarly research on the topic.

WEDDINGS WEREN'T ALWAYS LIKE THIS

American weddings were once informal affairs held in homes or at community events, like barn raisings or corn husking bees. *Source: Howard, Vicki. Brides, Inc.: American Weddings and the Business of Tradition. Philadelphia: University of Pennsylvania Press, 2008. Print.*

And the white wedding dress thing is garbage too.

Back then, white fabric was almost impossible to clean, so a white dress was only meant to be worn once. *Source: Baker, Lindsay. "The evolution of the wedding dress." BBC Culture. British Broadcasting Corporation, 5 May 2014. Web.*

It wasn't until Queen Victoria wore a white dress to her wedding that other brides began to copy her to show off their wealth. But even then, it was strictly for the well-to-do.

Even white wedding cakes were all about bragging. White sugar back then was so expensive, it was basically edible bling. *Source: Wilson, Carol. "Wedding Cake: A Slice of History." Gastronomica: The Journal of Critical Food Studies 5.2 (2005): 69-72. Web.*

THE WEDDING INDUSTRY BLEEDS COUPLES DRY

Even if a couple isn't rich, they'll be pushed into spending well beyond their means by a parasitic industry.

DR. VICKI HOWARD
Department of History
HARTWICK COLLEGE

DR. VICKI HOWARD,

Author of *Brides Incorporated*
Dept. of History, Hartwick College:

"Weddings used to be simple affairs, but then bridal magazines encouraged brides to marry like the wealthy, and created a wedding industry of unrelated products like silverware, gifts for the home, and even early wedding gowns.

"It was the birth of an entire industry, and now the cost of weddings keeps skyrocketing."

The wedding industry cheats people.

It systematically overcharges young couples just because they can. One study found that a majority of flower shops, photographers, and cake shops, charged more for a wedding than they did for a birthday party of the same size. It's called the wedding tax. *Source: "Do Vendors Charge More for Weddings than Other Events?" Bride.net. 18 Jul. 2010. Web.*

How do they get away with it?

Doesn't help that this culture's spending is now so pervasive, if you don't do it, your family will be pissed.

Spending all that on extravagance doesn't make couples "stronger" either.

Researchers at Emery University found that the more you spend on your wedding, the more likely your marriage will end in divorce. *Source: Khazan, Olga. "The Divorce-Proof Marriage." The Atlantic. Atlantic Media, 14 Oct. 2014. Web.*

Nobody you pay to help plan your wedding gives two craps if you stay together or not.

IT AIN'T REALLY ABOUT "EVERLASTING LOVE" EITHER

Science says your feelings are almost certain to change.

Sorry.

Isn't it weird that our culture is so obsessed with eternal love?

In America, we basically worship the concept of romantic love.

We make movies about it. We write poems to it. Heck, love is the most popular word in song lyrics. *Source: Schnoebelen, Tyler. "We've lost that lovin' feelin'." Corpus Linguistics. 22 Apr. 2016. Web.*

We're not counting function words. But the fact is, for most human history, love was considered a temporary emotion that had nothing to do with marriage. In fact, loving your spouse was once considered weird and irresponsible. *Source: "How marriage has changed over centuries." The Week. Michael Wolfe, 1 Jun. 2013. Web.*

In the second century, a Roman politician was expelled from the Senate for kissing his wife in public. *Source: Howard, Vicki. Brides, Inc.: American Weddings and the Business of Tradition. Philadelphia: University of Pennsylvania Press, 2008. Print.*

And, in the twelfth century, a famous treatist declared: "Love can have no place between husband and wife." *Source: Capellanus, Andreas. De Amore (The Art of Courtly Love.) 12th Cent.*

And let's not forget Benjamin Franklin, who said: "Love considered merely a passion, will naturally have but a short duration." *Source: Franklin, Benjamin. Reflections on Courtship and Marriage: in Two Letters to a Friend. Wherein a Practicable Plan is laid down for Obtaining and Securing Conjugal Felicity. Philadelphia: 1746. Web.*

On the other hand, Ben was kinda weird. Over a dozen skeletons were recently found in his basement—and nobody knows why they're there... *Source: Schultz, Colin. "Why Was Benjamin Franklin's Basement Filled with Skeletons?" Smithsonian.com. Smithsonian Institution, 3 Oct. 2013. Web.*

Anyway, what did they think love was for?

STEPHANIE COONTZ,

**Historian and Professor at
Evergreen State College
Author of *Marriage, A History:
How Love Conquered Marriage:***

"Love was a very frivolous, irresponsible distraction from the real business of marriage.

"For thousands of years, marriage was about making economic and political deals, military treaties, expanding the family labor force, and it was considered absolutely weird to do such important business for love. But about 200 years ago, some people began to insist that we should let young people make their own decisions, and we should let them make them on the basis of love."

Sound better? Sure.

But our modern concept of love is just as weird. In many ways, we take it way too seriously— beginning with the poet Samuel Taylor Coleridge who declared: "To be happy in married life, you must have a soul mate." *Source: Coleridge, Samuel Taylor. "Letter to a Young Lady, 1822." Letters, Conversations, and Recollections of S.T. Coleridge, vol. II. Ed. Thomas Allsop. London: Edward Moxon, Dover Street, 1836. 86-101. Web.*

Yeah. He coined the term "soul mate."

And we ran with that shiz. Today our dominant cultural narrative of love is that somewhere out there, everyone has a missing "other half," a single perfect counterpart, the mythical *one*.

This whole idea is complete nonsense.

LET'S DO THE MATH

About half the world's population is female, so for any given man, there are roughly 3.5 billion potential soul mates alive on Earth today. Now, let's assume he thinks soul mates are detected via eye contact. Let's also assume this man makes eye contact with a dozen new people every day. Multiply that by 365 days a year, and it will take 800,000 years for him to find his soul mate. He'll only meet her in one out of every 10,000 lifetimes.

OK. Maybe you think the soul mate thing is just a metaphor. But it's a metaphor that's hurting your very real relationships. *Source: Knee, C. Raymond. "Implicit Theories of Relationships: Assessment and Prediction of Romantic Relationship Initiation, Coping, and Longevity." Journal of Personality and Social Psychology 74.2 (1998): 360-70. Web.*

One study found that couples that believe in "destiny" and "soul mates" break up sooner than those that believe that relationships need to grow and change. *Source: Knee, C. Raymond. "Implicit Theories of Relationships: Assessment and Prediction of Romantic Relationship Initiation, Coping, and Longevity." Journal of Personality and Social Psychology 74.2 (1998): 360-70. Web.*

OBSESSION? FASCINATION? BUTTERFLIES IN YOUR STOMACH?

Hate to break it to you, but that's all part of a phenomenon called "limerence." It's a term that means intense involuntary infatuated love.

And you won't feel it forever.

Researchers say that limerence lasts, on average, just eighteen months to three years. *Source: Marshall, Andrew G. "That crazy little thing called love." The Guardian. Guardian Media Group, 13 Dec. 2003. Web.*

The biggest mistake our culture makes about love is when we connect a temporary feeling to a permanent union. The strongest relationships are between two people who understand that love, like all emotions, can grow and change, and sometimes even fade.

Now, your love might not fade. But it's important to accept that it *could*. Thinking that all love is eternal and butterflies are forever is straight-up fantasy. Realistic marriages can and do last, you just gotta prepare for what's gonna happen when the butterflies fly away.

And here's a real shocker:

DIVORCE IS GOOD

Our culture's fear of divorce is totally ridiculous.

Politicians and the media constantly talk as though divorces mere existence were a threat to society.

You've heard the saying: Half of all marriages end in divorce.

Bupkis!

Properly calculated, divorce rates in the U.S. have never exceeded 41 percent. And after peaking in the late '70s and early '80s, the divorce rate has actually gone down over the years. *Source: Hurley, Dan. Divorce Rate: It's Not as High as You Think. New York Times. The New York Times Company, 19 Apr. 2005. Web.*

Here's the key thing: A divorce doesn't mean a happy marriage is over. It means a *bad* one is.

In the old days, to get a divorce, you often needed both spouses present. You also needed to establish fault. So, if you wanted a boring old amicable divorce, you were forced to lie to a judge. *Source: Coontz, Stephanie. Marriage, a History: How Love Conquered Marriage. New York: Peguin, 2006. Print.*

This was particularly bad for women, because in many states, domestic violence wasn't considered grounds for divorce...so they could become trapped in abusive marriages. In some states, like Mississippi, that's still the case. *Source: "Mississippi not adding domestic violence as grounds for divorce." The Clarion Ledger. Nathan Edwards, 21 Apr. 2016. Web.*

But all that changed in 1969, thanks to Ronald Reagan. *Source: Wilcox, W. Bradford. "The Evolution of Divorce." National Affairs. National Affairs Inc., Fall 2009. Web.*

As governor of California, he introduced "no fault divorce," a revolutionary innovation that made it far easier for folks to separate.

The concept soon spread to other states, and by some estimates, reduced cases of female suicide by 20 percent. *Source: Stevenson, Betsey and Wolfers, Justin. "Bargaining in the Shadow of the Law: Divorce Laws and Family Distress." The National Bureau of Economic Research. Dec. 2003. Web.*

That's why divorce rates rose in the '70s—not because society was crumbling, but because divorce was finally available to the people who really needed it.

WHAT ABOUT THE KIDS?

Yeah, divorce can be tough on the little ones. But you know what's also tough on kids? Unhappy homes.

Research says that kids tend to do worse when surrounded by constant parental conflict. *Source: Coiro, Mary Jo and Morrison, Donna Ruane. "Parental Conflict and Marital Disruption: Do Children Benefit When High-Conflict Marriages Are Dissolved?" Journal of Marriage and the Family 6.1 (1999): 626-637. Web.*

And in many high-discord families, kids experience relief after separation. *Source: Arkowitz, Hal and Lilienfeld, Scott O. "Is Divorce Bad for Children?" Scientific American. Nature Publishing Group, 1 Mar. 2013. Web.*

HERE'S THE IMPORTANT THING...

For some couples, divorce is the right choice, and to them it represents freedom. It's a critical social right.

Marriages that last a lifetime are awesome. But marriages that last a decade, five years, or even just a few months, those can be wonderful and have value, too.

We shouldn't stigmatize them.

Remember limerence? Feelings do change. And, hey, hopefully *your* marriage will last a long, long time. But, if it doesn't, well, there's good news: Divorce is an option.

The pressure we put on marriage and weddings is insane. You're asking yourself to feel the same way about a person for the rest of your life. You're throwing a huge, expensive party for all your friends *and* it's a weird contract signing where you're promising to file joint tax returns.

Yeah, OK, it's tradition. But it's a tradition that's gotten a little out of hand.

The wedding isn't important.

The people are.

EPISODE SIXTEEN

ADAM RUINS
MALLS

DIRECTOR: LAURA MURPHY
ORIGINAL AIR DATE: SEPTEMBER 13, 2016

Shopping malls! A retreat for bored parents and antsy teens. They were created as tax loopholes for greedy developers. Outlet stores are just as nefarious. And don't get us started on nutrient supplements and eyeglasses manufacturers. No, wait. Please *do* get us started!

DID YOU KNOW:

VICTORIA'S SECRET WAS ORIGINALLY MARKETED TO MEN AS A SEXY PLACE WHERE THEY COULD BUY LINGERIE FOR THEIR WIVES AND GIRLFRIENDS.

Source: Barr, Naomi. "Happy Ending, Right?" Slate. Graham Holdings Company, 30 Oct. 2013. Web.

THE MALL WAS NOT DESIGNED TO BE A HAPPY PLACE FOR YOU

And there are way too many of them.

It all started in 1956, when an Austrian architect named Victor Gruen invented the modern mall. *Source: "The Gruen Effect." Prod. Avery Trufelman. 99% Invisible. KALW, San Francisco, 5 May 2015. Web.*

Gruen wanted to create an indoor town square where people could not only shop, but live, work, and build their community. He envisioned a utopia.

But his beautiful dream was corrupted by greedy developers. In the '50s, a legal loophole turned new developments into tax shelters...and nothing sheltered more taxes than malls. *Source: Hanchett, Thomas W. "US Tax Policy and the Shopping-Center Boom of the 1950s and 1960s." The American Historical Review 101.4 (1996): 1082-1110. Web.*

As a result, there was virtually no way to lose money building them.

By the '70s, they had built huge numbers of malls all across America, because of this loophole. Way more than anyone needs.

OUTLETS SUCK, TOO

Outlets are designed to make you think you're getting one over on the big corporations. As though you can get major discounts because brands make mistakes sewing the clothes or stocking their inventory.

Not true.

The truth is, the goods at outlets aren't factory rejects at all, they're just cheap, low quality clothes that the retailer is pretending are overstock.

Some estimate that 85 percent of clothes sold at outlets were actually manufactured exclusively for the outlets. *Source: Lieber, Chavie. "Buyer Beware: What You're Actually Getting at Outlet Stores." Racked. Vox Media, 8 Oct. 2014. Web.*

Gap openly admits that at their outlets, the clothing is 100 percent intentionally manufactured. Think about it: There are over 12,000 outlet stores throughout the U.S. How could factories be making enough "mistakes" to stock them all? *Source: Humphers, Linda. "2014 Outlet Tenant Report." Value Retail News. International Council of Shopping Centers, Mar. 2014. Web.*

THEN WHY ARE THE CLOTHES SO DEEPLY DISCOUNTED?

Because they're not.

At outlets, the MSRP (Manufacturer's Suggested Retail Price) is usually a fake number that the store makes up to make it look like the garment was once worth a lot—but in reality—it's a seven dollar dress, and they're selling it for seven dollars.

To get these prices, clothing made for outlets is also of noticeably lower quality. *Source: Tressler, Colleen. "Outlet Shopping: Getting Your Money's Worth." Consumer Information. Federal Trade Commission, 20 Mar. 2014. Web.*

Luxury brands often outsource their outlet merchandise to cheaper manufacturers, then slap on the fancy label. *Source: Randles, Jonathan. "Gap, Saks Sued For Duping Outlet Store Shoppers." Law360. LexisNexis, 20 Aug. 2014. Web.*

The question is: How can they get away with that?

DR. LAURA MCANDREWS,

**Assistant Professor of
Product Design and Development
University of Georgia:**

Dr. Laura McAndrews: "Honestly, this is an open secret in the industry. When I was at the Gap and product development, we never communicated with the outlet team. We were completely different supply chains: different yarns, different fabrics, even different factories. We basically were a different company."

How can they call it an outlet store?

Dr. Laura McAndrews: "Ultimately you can call anything an outlet or a factory store. The term has no meaning."

And as it turns *out,* outlet stores are so deceptive that four senators have asked the FDC to investigate them. *Source: "Sens. & Rep. to FTC: Outlet Stores May Be Misleading Customers." U.S. Senate, 30 Jan. 2014. Web.*

Dr. Laura McAndrews: "Frankly, traditional retailers aren't much better. You can't believe anything you read on a label. Clothing today is made so quickly and so cheaply, they're basically designed to fall apart. Fast fashion is killing the clothing industry."

Despite what they want you to think, you're not getting a deal at the outlets. You're paying full price for crap.

That includes whatever supplement store is attached to the place.

Because guess what?

SUPPLEMENTS CAN KILL YOU

Supplements are a completely unregulated game of Russian roulette.

And we know what you've heard:

"People use supplements all the time to lose weight or bulk up, or improve their health. You know, I read somewhere that 50 percent of Americans take supplements."

Well, that's a big problem, because supplements have been found to contain illicit and dangerous chemicals like undisclosed allergens, steroids, and even Viagra. *Source: Morin, Monte. "Undisclosed soy prompts voluntary recall, FDA says." Los Angeles Times. tronc, Inc., 21 Mar. 2013. Web. Source: Woolhouse, Megan. "Hidden hazards in bodybuilding products." Boston Globe. Boston Globe Media Partners, LLC, 17 Oct. 2009. Web. Source: "Hidden Risks of Erectile Dysfunction 'Treatments' Sold Online." Consumer Updates. U.S. Food and Drug Administration, 21 Feb. 2009. Web.*

And no, nobody is checking what goes into supplements. Before they hit the shelves, literally no one does. Anything could be in those bottles. *Source: Skerrett, Patrick J. "FDA needs stronger rules to ensure the safety of dietary supplements." Harvard Health Blog. Harvard Medical School, 2 Feb. 2012. Web.*

QUACK DOCTORING NEVER REALLY WENT AWAY

Back in the early 1900s, quack doctors could put anything in a bottle and call it medicine. *Source: Stromberg, Joseph. "What's in Century-Old 'Snake Oil' Medicines? Mercury and Lead." Smithsonian.com. Smithsonian Institution, 8 Apr. 2013. Web.*

So, to stop these charlatans from straight up killing people, we regulated the drug industry.

But those standards were never applied to supplements. And in 1994, the industry lobbied Congress to cripple the FDA's ability to investigate them. *Source: "Unregulated Dietary Supplements." New York Times. The New York Times Company, 19 Sep. 1998. Web. And now we're back to the bad old days when any bozo can put whatever they want in a bottle and sell it. The only thing that's changed is the facial hair.*

Any big dumb ape can mix together whatever crazy chemicals he wants, call it a "proprietary blend," and no one will stand between him and the store shelves.

IT'S NOT JUST THE BONER PILLS AND THE CRAZY MEATHEAD STUFF

Even herbal supplements like ginseng, ginkgo biloba, and Echinacea, have their own problem: plant fraud.

A study of DNA-tested herbal supplements found that a third of them contain no trace of the advertised plant. *Source: O'Connor, Anahad. "Herbal Supplements Are Often Not What They Seem." New York Times. The New York Times Company, 3 Nov. 2013. Web. Research showed instead, they contained fillers like powdered rice, wheat, and even laxatives.*

So, who's checking this garbage?

Well, there are 15,000 supplement manufacturers...but the FDA only conducts 400 inspections a year. And when they do inspect them, manufacturers fail 60 percent of the time. *Source: Kapoor, Akshay, and Joshua M. Sharfstein. "Breaking the gridlock: Regulation of dietary supplements in the United States." Drug Testing and Analysis (2015).*

DR. JOSHUA SHARFSTEIN,
Former Deputy Commissioner of the FDA
Professor at Johns Hopkins:

Dr. Joshua Sharfstein: "The truth is, the FDA has so little authority here, the agency can't take action to protect the public until after someone is hurt. *Source: Seamon, Matthew J., and Kevin A. Clauson. "Ephedra: yesterday, DSHEA, and tomorrow—a ten year perspective on the Dietary Supplement Health and Education Act of 1994. Journal of Herbal Pharmacotherapy 5.3 (2005): 67-86."*

"One herbal product, ephedra, was linked to more than one hundred deaths. But because of industry pressure and a weak law, the agency took nearly ten years to get it off the market."

But this crap is sold at drug stores next to actual drugs.

Dr. Joshua Sharfstein: "And drugs are well regulated by the FDA, but when it comes to dietary supplements, the agency literally does not know what is in the bottles that are on the shelves...Until the FDA has the authority to know what's actually in dietary supplements, consumers will continue to be exposed to unnecessary risks."

This problem is only going to get worse, because supplements are a thirty-two-billion-dollar yearly industry. *Source: Lariviere, David. "Nutritional Supplements Flexing Muscles As Growth Industry." Forbes. Forbes, Inc., 18 Apr. 2013. Web.*

IF YOU WANNA GET IN ON IT, YOU CAN

The *Adam Ruins Everything* producers looked into it. They found a supplement company willing to manufacture a formula Adam came up with for less than 4,000 dollars, even though he's a comedian with no medical training. The only reason we didn't do it is the network said it was too dangerous.

Go figure.

The FDA knows it's a problem, but because of these laws, they have no authority to stop it.

Unfortunately, until the law is changed, millions of Americans will keep taking largely unregulated products full of mystery ingredients that—worst case scenario—could kill them.

NOT EVEN YOUR EYEGLASSES ARE SAFE FROM QUACKERY

You might think you're eyeballing the latest styles, but in reality, the frames are probably the same. And they're likely from the same company.

Think about this for a second: Even the most basic pair of glasses can cost around 400 dollars. That's as much as a phone. Haven't you ever wondered why a simple piece of plastic is the same price as a miracle of technology?

Well, as it turns out, many major glasses and sunglasses brands are controlled by a single company: Luxottica. *Source: Swanson, Ana. "Meet the Four-Eyed, Eight-Tentacled Monopoly That is Making Your Glasses So Expensive." Forbes. Forbes, Inc., 10 Sep. 2014. Web.*

Many have accused them of being a monopoly.

And because they control both luxury brands and cheap brands, they can charge pretty much whatever they want for either.

Luxottica uses that power to drive up the price of glasses for everybody, sometimes charging as much as twenty times what they cost to produce. *Source: "Sticker Shock: Why Are Glasses So Expensive?" Rep. Lesley Stahl. 60 Minutes. CBS, 16 Jun. 2013. Web.*

And it's not just prescription glasses.

Ray-Bans used to be bargain mass-market sunglasses, worn by everyone from jazz men to presidents, to president jazz man.

Back in 1999, Luxottica bought the brand and raised the price to over 150 dollars a pair. Quintuple what they were. *Source: Goodman, Andrew. "There's More To Ray-Ban And Oakley Than Meets The Eye." Forbes. Forbes, Inc., 16 Jul. 2014. Web.*

Fun fact: Almost half of Luxottica's glasses are manufactured in China and India. *Source: Arends, Brett. "Are Designer Sunglasses Worth the Price?" Wall Street Journal. News Corp., 22 Jul. 2010. Web.*

NOPE. CAN'T JUST GO TO A DIFFERENT STORE

Luxottica also owns almost all the major glasses stores too. That includes Lens Crafters, Pearl Vision, Sears Optical, Target Optical, and Sunglass Hut.

Which means that the few brands they don't own are forced to obey their demands.

For example, when Oakley tried to dispute Luxottica's pricing, Luxottica retaliated by dropping them from all their stores. Oakley's stock price collapsed. And Luxottica swooped in and bought them out. *Source: "Sticker Shock: Why Are Glasses So Expensive?" Rep. Lesley Stahl. 60 Minutes. CBS, 16 Jun. 2013. Web.*

Luxottica has so much power that when a company didn't play by their rules, they brought them to the brink of destruction, then took over that company.

What sucks is that for 75 percent of Americans, glasses are a medical necessity. Too bad Luxottica also owns the second largest eye insurance company in America. *Source: "Media." EyeMed Vision Care. 2014.*

That means it's possible for your optometrist, your insurance company, the factory that makes your frames, and the store that sells them to you, to all be owned by the same company.

Fun!

Basically, they can just rip consumers off.

"Everything is worth what people are ready to pay."

That might sound cynical as hell, but, it's also a real thing that their CEO said to *60 Minutes.*

The fact is, most of these glasses could just be labeled Luxottica. But they're not, because what Luxottica is really selling you is the illusion of choice.

AS NOT SEEN ON TV

The episode was filmed at a mall in the Eagle Rock neighborhood of Los Angeles, which is still very much in operation. So it's a long way from becoming one of the spruced-up community centers that have been fashioned out of abandoned malls anytime soon.

The Mall

THE UPSIDE IS...

Now that we shop online, Luxottica has lost a lot of power. A ton of independent retailers are going around them and selling to consumers directly.

And!

Malls are dying!

That tax loophole we mentioned led to the construction of so many unneeded malls that the market was oversaturated. And now these crummy, claustrophobic shopping centers are failing. And good riddance.

Instead, cities all over America are building outdoor town squares filled with restaurants, local businesses, public space, and even housing.

Yay!

ADAM RUINS
ANIMALS

DIRECTOR: LAURA MURPHY
ORIGINAL AIR DATE: SEPTEMBER 20, 2016

Are you a "cat person" or a "dog person"? Actually...don't answer that. It doesn't matter. Because purebred dogs are genetic monsters created by bored Victorians, domestic cats are overpopulated lethal killing machines that threaten other animals, and wild animal trophy hunting can actually help endangered species. Join us, won't you?

THIS IS GONNA BE RUFF

Purebred dogs are the worst.

Not only are purebred dogs riddled with genetic disease, dog breeds aren't even a real thing. We made them up.

We talk about dog breeds as though God created them that way.

And it was thought every mutt was just a mix of different purebreeds. But that's backwards. Mutts are dogs in their natural state. Humans have lived with domesticated dogs for over 10,000 years, but so-called "purebred" dogs didn't even exist until just 150 years ago. *Source: "Evolution of the Dog." PBS.org. Public Broadcasting Station, 2001. Web.*

So where did they come from?

Pure breeding is a form of genetic manipulation humans made up just to amuse ourselves.

AS IS OFTEN THE CASE, BLAME ENGLAND

In nineteenth century Victorian England, eugenics was all the rage, and competitive dog breeding became a weird fancy fad. *Source: Pemberton, Neil and Michael Worboys. "The surprising history of Victorian dog shows." BBC History Magazine. The British Broadcasting Corporation, Jun. 2009. Web.*

Once these Dr. Frankensteins were satisfied, they dubbed their little monsters "pure breeds," and used kennel clubs to enforce their bizarre standards.

This is a corgi:

Source: "Official Standard of the Pembroke Welsh Corgi." American Kennel Club, 13 Jun. 1972. Web.

A corgi is ten to twelve inches tall, with a foxy head, wide and a flat skull. *Source: "Official Standard of the Pembroke Welsh Corgi." American Kennel Club, 13 Jun. 1972. Web.*

That's all a corgi really is, an arbitrary definition made up by a weirdo.

PUREBREDS AREN'T HEALTHIER, EITHER

When you hear purebred, you should think inbred.

Kennel clubs prohibit purebred dogs from mating outside their breed, and often they're mated to members of their own family, making the average pug as inbred as an Austrian duke. *Source: Maldarelli, Claire. "Although Purebred Dogs Can Be Best in Show, Are They Worst in Health?" Scientific American. Nature Publishing Group, 21 Feb. 2014. Web.*

And as everyone knows, inbreeding ain't natural.

The sad truth is, purebred dogs suffer from disturbingly high rates of genetic disease. It's because of a problem called the "genetic bottleneck."

DR. KIRK LOHMUELLER,

Professor of Evolution at UCLA:

Dr. Kirk Lohmueller: "Here's the problem with pure breeding. When species breed in the wild, they can exist in large populations and can mate randomly. This ensures a nice healthy distribution of genetic variation.

"But when humans started pure breeding dogs, they had them mate over and over again with their relatives to get a specific look. When we artificially limited the gene pool in that way, we created a genetic bottleneck. As the same small gene pool is spread between more and more dogs, diseases that would normally be rare become inevitable."

Wouldn't a good breeder only mate the healthy ones?

Dr. Kirk Lohmueller: "Well, you can try. But if you don't increase the size of the gene pool, you're gonna keep creating abnormal dogs. Tiny physical defects like smaller noses, for example, might get worse and worse over time, until it becomes impossible for the dog to breathe. The reality is, pure breeding leads to unhealthy dogs."

And those diseases are real serious.

Sixty percent of Golden Retrievers die of cancer. *Source: Beck, Melinda. "When Cancer Comes With a Pedigree." Wall Street Journal. Dow Jones & Company, 4 May 2010. Web.* An estimated 95 percent of King Charles Spaniels have skulls that are too small for their brains. *Source: "Chiari-like malformation (CM) and syringomyelia (SM)." Canine Inherited Disorders Database. Atlantic Veterinary College, University of Prince Edward Island, 2011. Web.* Pugs' faces are so flat, they reverse sneeze. *Source: Roedler, Frauke S., Sabine Pohl, and Gerhard U. Oechtering. "How does severe brachycephaly affect dog's lives? Results of a structured preoperative owner questionnaire." The Veterinary Journal 198.3 (2013): 606-610.* Great Danes are so huge, they get bone tumors from supporting their own weight. *Source: "Dogs That Changed the World: Selective Breeding Problems." PBS.org. Public Broadcasting Station, 16 Sep. 2010. Web.*

And as for toy breeds, have you ever seen a little tiny dog that looked happy? They know there's something wrong with them, and they know that we did it to them.

Let's take a look at the English bulldog.

The bulldog was once a proud breed, but a century of extreme breeding has ruined them.

Their noses are so squashed, they can barely breathe. Their heads are so big, they're usually born by C-section. Their tails can become ingrown. They basically all have hip dysplasia, and their average life expectancy is six years. *Source: Denizet-Lewis, Benoit. "Can the Bulldog Be Saved?" New York Times Magazine. The New York Times Company, 22 Nov. 2011. Web.* Frankly, it's surprising these dogs can even survive.

The sad part is, all the bulldogs' problems would be solved if breeders would just allow them to cross breed, but they won't because then they wouldn't look like bulldogs.

Our insistence that these dogs live up to our arbitrary standards is causing them to get sick and die. As cute as you think the bulldog is, the fact that it exists at all is borderline animal abuse.

That doesn't mean you shouldn't get a dog. Just skip the breeder and the pet store and head on down to your local shelter to get a cute little mutt. It'll be 100 percent all natural dog and, better yet, you'll be giving a home to a pup that really needs one.

Speaking of helping animals…

DON'T FEED STRAY CATS

Feeding stray cats doesn't help animals. In fact, it helps kill billions of animals every year.

The feral cat population has spiraled out of control and it's all our fault.

There are over seventy million pet cats in the U.S. *Source: "U.S. Pet Ownership Statistics." American Veterinary Medical Association, 2012. Web. We love them, we cuddle them, and we Snapchat the hell out of them.*

Unfortunately, some people also let those cats outside.

And while they're outside, those cats breed.

The average cat can give birth to as many as twelve kittens a year. *Source: "Shelter Intake and Surrender: Pet Statistics." American Society for the Prevention of Cruelty to Animals, 2016. Web.*

And their kittens are born feral. Put all of that together, and there are now as many as seventy million feral cats living in the U.S.

Basically, for every pet cat living inside, there's a feral cat living outside.

These cats live tragically short lives. They suffer from disease, they're hit by cars, and they get attacked by animals—including other cats. *Source: Nutter, Felicia B., Jay F. Levine, and Michael K. Stoskopf. "Reproductive capacity of free-roaming domestic cats and kitten survival rate." Journal of the American Veterinary Medical Association 225.9 (2004): 1399-1402.*

While indoor cats live about fifteen years, the average outdoor cat dies after just five. *Source: "Your Cat - Indoors or Out." Mobile Society for the Prevention of Cruelty to Animals, 2003. Web.*

Yeah. That's sad. But it's even worse for birds.

Cats kill birds whether or not they're hungry. Even if they've just been fed. *Source: Robertson, I. D. "Survey of predation by domestic cats." Australian Veterinary Journal 76.8 (1998): 551-554.*

A conservative estimate is that feral cats kill 1.3 billion birds a year. *Source: Loss, Scott R., Tom Will, and Peter P. Marra. "The impact of free-ranging domestic cats on wildlife of the United States." Nature Communications 4 (2013): 1396.* They've actually driven twenty bird species extinct. *Source: Medina, Félix M., et al. "A global review of the impacts of invasive cats on island endangered vertebrates." Global Change Biology 17.11 (2011): 3503-3510.*

Birds pollenate plants and distribute seeds, making them an essential part of the North American ecosystem. But cats aren't. In fact, they're an invasive species that's killing native ones.

Our love for cats is what caused this problem. Humans are the ones who brought cats to this country and let them outside. There are even entire groups of people devoted to supporting feral cat colonies.

As well-intentioned as these folks are, they're sustaining a population of unhealthy, unhappy animals that kills a billion birds a year.

So, what should we do? Let seventy million cats die? Murder them all to death?

There is no easy solution to this problem. If you have a cat, spay or neuter it, and please keep it inside. That's at least a start. But meanwhile, we need to face the fact that our love for animals, if we're not careful, can do more harm than good.

While we're on the topic of helping animals...

TROPHY HUNTING CAN REALLY HELP ENDANGERED ANIMALS

This argument is really counter intuitive and, frankly, kind of difficult to accept. But keep an open mind, because the evidence suggests that in specific situations, trophy hunting can really help endangered animals.

In Africa, animals like these are in desperate straits.

Here's how many are alive: Elephant, 470,000. African Lion: 20,000. Black rhino: 5,000. *Source: "African Elephant." World Wildlife Fund, 2016. Web.* "Black Rhino." World Wildlife Fund, 2016. Web. "Declining Lion." NationalGeographic.com. National Geographic Society, 2016. Web.

The real threat to these animals isn't trophy hunters. The real threats are loss of habitat and poaching. *Source: Platt, John R. "African Lion Populations Drop 42 Percent in Past 21 Years." Scientific American. Nature Publishing Group, 24 Jun. 2015. Web.*

Poachers are organized, they're ruthless, and they are decimating animal populations. In some countries, rhino horn is believed to cure cancer and even hangovers, and sells for 28,000 dollars a pound. That's more than gold or cocaine. *Source: Guilford, Gwynn. "Why Does a Rhino Horn Cost $300,000? Because Vietnam Thinks It Cures Cancer and Hangovers." The Atlantic. Atlantic Media Group, 15 May 2013. Web.*

Why don't the locals stop them?

Well, they're kinda busy, y'know, living their lives.

And just as harmful to animal populations is the habitat loss caused by farming. These animals are literally running out of places to live. So, some African nations came up with a plan. They took advantage of the existing demand for trophy hunting and used it to fund animal conservation.

In Namibia, revenue from trophy hunting is the main way they fund new wildlife conservancies. *Source: Lindsey, P. A., P. A. Roulet, and S. S. Romanach. "Economic and conservation significance of the trophy hunting industry in sub-Saharan Africa." Biological Conservation 134.4 (2007): 455-469.* And in South Africa, a portion of the proceeds from trophy hunting is given directly to local land owners, and that incentivizes them to give the rhinos land to live on and to protect them from poachers. *Source: Goldman, Jason G. "Can Trophy Hunting Actually Help Conservation?" Conservation Magazine. University of Washington, 15 Jan. 2014. Web.*

"But wait," you may be saying, "they're just being kept alive to be shot."

Absolutely true. But still, this system works. One third of all white rhinos in South Africa now live on private land, and their population has gone from just one hundred to more than 18,000. *Source: "White Rhino." World Wildlife Fund, 2016. Web.*

ROSIE COONEY,

Chair of Sustainable Use and Livelihood Specialist Group of the International Union for the Conservation of Nature:

Rosie Cooney: "It's true...trophy hunting can be a valuable part of conservation efforts, even if you find hunting distasteful. It's not the hunters running these programs, it's the government agencies, or sometimes even conservation groups themselves."

The hunters' motives don't really matter, the money they generate can really help the animals who need it. But how do I know the money is going to the right place?

Rosie Cooney: "Well, that's a good question. Like any program, where there's a lot of corruption or where things are badly managed, these programs don't work well at all. But that doesn't change the fact that when they are well managed, these programs can be a huge help for wildlife conservation. In Namibia, for example, 100 percent of the hunting concession fees goes straight to the local communities. It's been a huge success.

"Many countries are depending on this revenue to protect animals, to pay the game guards, to buy the vehicles. What happens if that money dries up? It's very easy for us in the developed world to judge how other countries should manage their animals. But should it be our decision, or should it be up to the communities who live with these animals every day? Hunting is a really important source of conservation revenue, even [in the U.S.]."

Hunting fees generate around 200 million dollars a year, which—for many states—is their primary source of conservation funding. *Source: U.S. Fish & Wildlife Service 2014.*

We know this is hard to comprehend. We love these animals so much we can't imagine any benefit coming from their deaths. It just seems wrong. But you know what's worse than one animal getting killed by a hunter? Hundreds of thousands being wiped out by poaching and loss of habitat. The truth is, in some nations, the regulated hunting of a few individuals is helping to save entire species.

AS NOT SEEN ON TV

Adam has a mutt named Indi who stops by the studio sometimes to spend the day in the writers' room. Not a purebred!

THE "CUTE" FACTOR

Cuteness is the emotion that makes us wanna nurture and protect things, so we just need to expand our notion of what we find cute. Like instead of genetically manipulating dogs for our own amusement, we should decide that we find all shapes and sizes of dog cute and rescue mutts from local shelters.

And instead of giving strays and feral cats all the attention, we need to think more about adorable songbirds—they're cute too, and they need our help.

Yes, elephants, rhinos, and lions need protection. But so do a lot of other less traditionally cute animals. For instance, the critically endangered American burying beetle: They bury rodent carcasses in the dirt, then lay their eggs in them, which helps plants grow. *Source: Ratcliffe, B.C. "Endangered American Burying Beetle Update." University of Nebraska State Museum, 1997. Web.*

If we decide they're cute enough to save, we can help preserve an important part of the ecosystem. So, let's cutify that beetle.

You can learn more about these disgusting adorable little guys at savethelittlebugs.org.

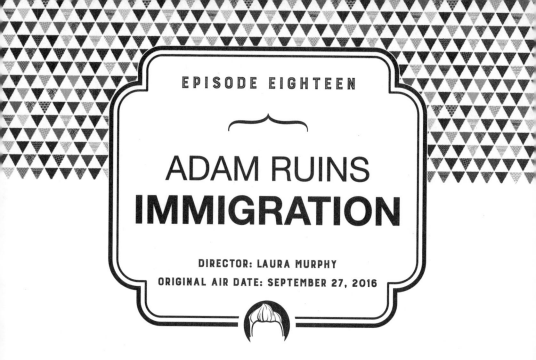

EPISODE EIGHTEEN

ADAM RUINS
IMMIGRATION

DIRECTOR: LAURA MURPHY
ORIGINAL AIR DATE: SEPTEMBER 27, 2016

Discussing immigration stirs up a ton of emotions. For. Against. Whatever is in-between. But, of course, everything you know is wrong. A
border wall wouldn't keep out illegal immigrants who overstay their
visas, racist mass deportations have historically led to disaster, and
immigration courts are a huge mess. *Hola!*

A WALL WON'T STOP ILLEGAL IMMIGRATION

The fact is, building a wall would actually increase the number of immigrants in America.

Just building a wall would be practically impossible.

It would have to stretch over 2,000 miles of rough terrain, cutting
through mountains, rivers, villages, and even people's homes. *Source:
U.S. Department of Homeland Security. U.S. Customs and Border Protection. Border in Miles.
Washington, 2016. Web.*

And all that destruction is monstrously expensive. Just building a wall
would cost between fifteen and twenty-five billion dollars. *Source: Drew,
Kate. "This is what Trump's border wall could cost US." CNBC. NBCUniversal Comcast, 9 Oct. 2015. Web.*

It would easily be one of the single most expensive pieces of infrastructure in American history, costing as much as twenty Hoover dams or NASA's entire annual budget. *Source: Granath, Bob. "'Reach for New Heights' — NASA Budget Unveiled for Fiscal Year 2016." NASA.gov. National Aeronautics and Space Administration, Feb. 2, 2015. Web.*

AS NOT SEEN ON TV ✂

The writers and researchers began pitching this episode before the 2016 primary. Donald Trump had been campaigning on a border wall, so immigration-related topics were very fresh on everyone's mind. At the time, they figured that Trump would fizzle out quickly, and worried the episode might feel stale or irrelevant by the time it aired months later. As it turns out, nothing could have been further from the truth. Gonzalo Cordova worked overtime writing a script that was heavily in Spanish, which the staff believed would make Abuela's character feel more realistic and give the story more power. The episode was eventually selected to be submitted for Emmy consideration. Better luck next year!

Not to mention the astronomical cost of staffing and maintaining the wall, which taxpayers like you and your children will be stuck paying forever.

Even just faking the wall for this episode was prohibitively expensive.

This isn't a "once it's built, it'll work" situation.

Increasing security at the border will never stop illegal immigration.

And that's because it's estimated that between 27 and 40 percent of all undocumented immigrants in America came here on planes. *Source: Greenberg, Joe. "Ramos: 40% of undocumented immigrants come by air." Politifact. Tampa Bay Times, 8 Sep. 2015. Web.*

These immigrants didn't sneak over the border. They came here legally through passport control, then just overstayed their visas. And guess what, the border wall's not gonna stop them because, reminder, planes can fly over walls.

IT WON'T STOP THE OTHER HALF OF ILLEGAL IMMIGRATION EITHER

That's because of a little something called "circular flow."

For decades, immigration to the U.S. had a circular flow—people would come, work for a bit, and then after they were done, go home to their families.

DOUGLAS S. MASSEY, PHD,

Professor of Sociology and Public Affairs, Princeton University:

Douglas S. Massey: "When the Reagan, Bush, and Clinton administrations drastically increased border enforcement in response to public opinion, they stopped that circular flow."

Not by keeping people out, but by keeping people in. As it got harder and harder to go back and forth, people crossing the border decided they were much better off just staying in the U.S.

Douglas S. Massey: "Ironically, this increase in border enforcement caused the number of undocumented immigrants living in the United States to skyrocket by 248 percent."

It's counterintuitive, but building a wall wouldn't stop people from coming in...it would actually stop them from going back.

Douglas S. Massey: "In fact, the whole idea of building a border wall is misguided. The Mexican economy is doing quite well right now, and population growth has slowed way down. So, there's not much pressure to immigrate. The number of illegal border crossings is actually at an all-time low." *Source: Massey, Douglas. "Donald Trump's Mexican Border Wall Is a Moronic Idea." Foreign Policy. The FP Group, 18 Aug. 2015. Web.*

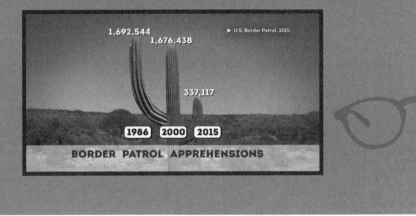

1,692,544
1,676,438
337,117
▶ U.S. Border Patrol, 2015.
1986 2000 2015
BORDER PATROL APPREHENSIONS

America already has what's likely the most militarized border between any two nations at peace. So, the real issue of immigration isn't the people coming in. The fact is, they're already here. Nearly one out of every thirty people in America is an unauthorized immigrant. *Source: "Unauthorized Immigrant Population Trends for States, Birth Countries and Regions." Pew Research Center, 11 Dec. 2014. Web.*

The only thing a wall stops is a discussion of actual solutions.

some heroes wear glasses

so many pocket squares, so little time

NO, DEPORTATION ISN'T THE ANSWER

Mass deportations always end in disaster.

America's deportation history is a disturbing cycle. *Source: "A Continent Divided: The U.S. – Mexico War." University of Texas Arlington Library Special Collections, 2016. Web.*

Our story begins in 1846, when President Polk provoked war with Mexico as an excuse to seize their land. *Source: "A Continent Divided: The U.S. – Mexico War." University of Texas Arlington Library Special Collections, 2016. Web.*

We're talking about how the U.S. straight up attacked Mexico and took millions of square miles of their land just because we could. *Source: Griswold del Castillo, Richard. "War's End: Treaty of Guadelupe Hidalgo." PBS.org. Public Broadcasting Service, 14 Mar. 2006. Web.*

President Polk's war seized land that now includes Texas, California, Nevada, Arizona, Wyoming, Colorado, Utah, and the rest.

Yeah, all these states were part of Mexico. The people who were living there were Mexican.

Then in 1930, President Herbert Hoover blamed those same Mexicans for the Great Depression. *Source: McGreevy, Patrick and Shelby Grad. "California law seeks history of Mexican deportations in textbooks." Los Angeles Times. tronc Inc., 1 Oct. 2015. Web.*

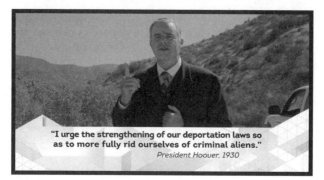

"I urge the strengthening of our deportation laws so as to more fully rid ourselves of criminal aliens."
President Hoover, 1930

Source: McGreevy, Patrick and Shelby Grad. "California law seeks history of Mexican deportations in textbooks." Los Angeles Times. tronc Inc., 1 Oct. 2015. Web.

During the '30s and '40s, local and state officials deported up to two million Mexicans. *Source: Florido, Adrian. "Mass Deportation May Sound Unlikely, But It's Happened Before." Code Switch. National Public Radio, 8 Sep. 2015. Web.*

And more than half of them were American citizens. *Source: Gross, Terry. "America's Forgotten History Of Mexican-American 'Repatriation.'" Fresh Air. National Public Radio, 10 Sep. 2015. Web.*

During this period, the U.S. deported nearly one million of our own citizens just because they had brown skin.

Soon after the deportations, World War II began. The United States changed their minds, and decided they needed Mexicans after all. Congress enacted the Bracero Program and welcomed Mexicans to the U.S. to fill jobs left behind by soldiers. *Source: "The Bracero Program: Bracero History Archive." UCLA Labor Center. University of California, 2014. Web.*

And then...

After a decade of inviting Mexicans to enter the U.S., in 1954, President Eisenhower declared take-backsies.

Source: Linthicum, Kate. "The dark, complex history of Trump's model for his mass deportation plan." Los Angeles Times. tronc Inc., 13 Nov. 2015. Web.

Changed our minds, we hate Mexicans again, let's get them all out of here and implement Operation Wetback. Source: Linthicum, Kate. "The dark, complex history of Trump's model for his mass deportation plan." Los Angeles Times. tronc Inc., 13 Nov. 2015. Web.

Not only were these programs explicitly racist, they were a human rights disaster.

Thousands of families were detained and separated, even crowded onto boats described as eighteen century slave ships. *Source: Peralta, Eyder. "It Came Up In The Debate: Here Are 3 Things To Know About 'Operation Wetback.'" The Two-Way. National Public Radio, 11 Nov. 2015. Web.* And those who went by sea were lucky. Eighty-eight braceros died after being left in the desert. *Source: Heer, Jeet. "Operation Wetback Revisited." The New Republic. Hamilton Fish V, 25 Apr. 2016. Web.*

Not only was this program unconscionably inhumane, it destroyed the image of America as a bastion of freedom and equality for a generation of Mexican Americans.

These mass deportation programs are one of the most shameful chapters in America's history. They solve nothing. Their only outcome was suffering and death.

AND OUR IMMIGRATION COURTS ARE A NIGHTMARE

It's not just pieces of it that are messed up—the entire system is one big judicial garbage fire.

All kinds of people are scooped up into these courts. Some were apprehended at the border or committed a crime, others were picked up for a minor traffic violation, and some just lost their paperwork.

Some came here legally...others not so much. The purpose of this court is to determine which is which.

Here's the problem: Less than 2 percent of what we spend on immigration annually is devoted to these courts. There are just fifty-eight immigration courts across the U.S., think about that. *Source: U.S. Department of Justice. Executive Office for Immigration Review. Office of the Chief Immigration Judge. Washington: 2016. Web.* We have thirty times as many Radio Shacks as we do immigration courts. *Source: Brustein, Joshua. After RadioShack Dies, There Will Still Be 1,000 Unchanged RadioShacks. Bloomberg Businessweek. Bloomberg L.P., 6 Feb. 2015. Web.*

And there are definitely more folks with immigration problems than there are people who need Blackberry holsters. The immigration courts currently have an insane backlog of 489,000 cases. *Source: "Immigration Court Backlog Tool." TRAC: Transactional Records Access Clearinghouse. Syracuse University, 2016. Web.*

This underfunded system has so few immigration judges that each one handles 1,500 cases a year, and unlike regular judges, they can actually be fired for not working fast enough. *Source: Saslow, Eli. "In a crowded immigration court, seven minutes to decide a family's future." Washington Post. Nash Holdings LLC, 2 Feb. 2014. Web.*

Even worse, the vast majority of respondents go through this system without a lawyer. Unlike regular, or—let's be frank—real courts, immigration courts do not provide lawyers...even to unaccompanied minors. *Source: Nzelibe, Uzoamaka Emeka. "Why are these children representing themselves in court?" Reuters. Thomson Reuters, 14 Jan. 2016. Web.*

Not to mention the severe language barrier. In some cases, interpreters are only available over the phone.

THIS ISN'T AN EXAGGERATION

Often it's much worse. Some detention centers are so remote, defendants can't even be physically present in court so the government conducts hearings via Skype or tele-video.

That means you can have a hearing where the judge is in the courtroom, the translator's talking over the phone, and the defendant is on a webcam. This is really happening in immigration courtrooms all across America right now. And it's no surprise that under this cockamamie process, huge mistakes happen constantly.

PROFESSOR JACQUELINE STEVENS,

Department of Political Science, Northwestern University:

Professor Jacqueline Stevens: "This system regularly deports American citizens....In fact, in 2009, I got to know a man named Mark Little, he is a U.S. citizen with mental disabilities who was deported in what's called a 'mass removal.' *Source: Finnegan, William. "The Deportation Machine." New Yorker. Conde Nast, 29 Apr. 2013. Web.* The judge asked a group of thirty men over tele-video to raise their hands if they objected to being deported. The judge recorded seeing no hands."

When Little later told them he was born in North Carolina, no one listened.

Professor Jacqueline Stevens: "He was deported to Mexico. When officials there discovered he wasn't a Mexican citizen, he was deported yet again to Honduras. And they deported him to Guatemala."

Police in Guatemala finally found Mark Little sleeping on a park bench thousands of miles from home.

Professor Jacqueline Stevens: "When he arrived in Atlanta, they detained him again....[This is] shockingly common. According to my research, more than 20,000 U.S. citizens have been detained or deported since 2003."

This system is so broken, natural-born American citizens are deported all the time. Whether you're conservative or liberal, or somewhere in between, you have to face the fact that what our immigration system does to people is contrary to every American value.

HERE'S THE BOTTOM LINE

Undocumented immigrants are an integral part of making American society function. They contribute to the economy and they even pay into social security, even though they'll never receive benefits from it. *Source: "Undocumented Immigrants' State & Local Tax Contributions." Institute on Taxation and Economic Policy, 24 Feb. 2016. Web. Source: Davidson, Adam. "Do Illegal Immigrants Actually Hurt the U.S. Economy?" New York Times. The New York Times Company, 12 Feb. 2013. Web.* Despite all that, we still put them through a crazy system we know doesn't work.

They're part of this country, like anyone else. Just because we can't agree on politics, that doesn't mean they're not American.

ADAM RUINS
HOUSING

DIRECTOR: MATTHEW POLLOCK
ORIGINAL AIR DATE: OCTOBER 4, 2016

Contrary to what most of us grew up hearing, homeownership is a terrible idea, housing share programs hurt city dwellers, and trying help the homeless can make the problem worse.

BUYING HOUSES IS NOT "GOOD INVESTING"

A lot of people who shop for homes would actually be better off renting.

For almost a century, Americans have been taught that home ownership is the ultimate middle-class ideal.

But the fact is, for millions of us, this is a dream that's not worth chasing.

Buying a home does not grant you freedom.

When you rent, can move whenever you want. But after you buy, you're sort of stuck.

It's even been shown that higher rates of home ownership lead to higher unemployment for exactly this reason. *Source: Oswald, Andrew J. "A Conjecture on the Explanation for High Unemployment in the Industrialized Nations: Part I." Coventry: University of Warwick, 1996. Web.*

It doesn't make financial sense. Instead of paying rent to a landlord, you'll be paying a mortgage to a bank. How is that any different?

Oh, banks don't fix anything. That's the difference.

Often, buying doesn't give you any more stability than renting—you're just paying a different jerk. And, for the first few years, you're not even building equity...you're just paying off interest.

Realtors and financial pundits would have you believe that if you don't buy a home, you're an idiot.

But what they don't tell you is that buying a house can actually be a really risky investment.

Real financial experts recommend that you always diversify, splitting your money between lots of different investments, so if one of them goes south, you don't lose everything. But if you sink your entire net worth into one pile of wood and nails, and the housing market tanks—like it did in 2008—you lose everything.

And the crash of 2008 was not a "blip." People always say the housing market goes up on average, but that just isn't true.

One of the world's foremost housing economists found that when you adjust for inflation, over the last century, the housing market hasn't risen at all. *Source: Housel, Morgan. "Why your home is not a good investment." USA Today. Gannett Company, 10 May 2014. Web.* Not to mention the "phantom costs."

Phantom costs are the hidden expenses of home ownership we ignore when we rush to buy.

Home insurance. Property taxes. Closing costs. Repairs.

In the first two years, the average home owner spends more than 14,000 dollars on improvements, which can more than wipe out whatever little profit you make. *Source: Sichelman, Lew. "The hidden costs of homeownership." Los Angeles Times. Tronc, Inc., 2 May 2010. Web.*

RAMIT SETHI,

Personal Finance Expert,
New York Times Bestselling Author:

Ramit Sethi: "You know, the truth is...a lot of Americans actually reduce their net worth instead of increasing it when they buy a house. That's because they don't factor in taxes, maintenance, insurance, even repairing a roof, and that can put them behind instead of ahead."

So should people just always rent? Maybe. Renting is actually a much better deal than most people think.

Ramit Sethi: "A lot of people are gonna tell you, you're throwing money away on rent. Don't listen to them. Just think about it, the landlord has to take on all the risks. If the price of the house goes down, they're stuck with it. If something breaks, they have to fix it. Meanwhile, you live in that house, you pay a nominal rent, and if you need to pack up and leave, you can do it."

That doesn't mean you should never buy a house.

Ramit Sethi: "No, look, buying a house can make sense for some people, but just remember, this is the biggest financial decision of your life. So, make sure that you can afford it, make sure that you can put 20 percent down, and make sure you're gonna live there for at least 10 years. And, please, talk to a financial expert before you buy, not a real estate agent." *Source: Bostock, Mike, Carter, Shan and Tse, Archie. "Is It Better to Rent or Buy?" New York Times. The New York Times Company, 1 Apr. 2016. Web.*

EVER WONDER WHY...

Ever wondered why the government gives you a tax break on your mortgage? The fact is, they probably shouldn't. Every year the United States government gives out nearly 70 billion dollars in mortgage interest deductions.

Most people think that money helps hard working Americans buy homes of their own. But the fact is, it doesn't. Most of that money goes straight to the people who need it the least: rich folks.

You're only eligible for that tax break if you itemize your taxes, and most people don't. In layman's terms, that means over 75 percent of that sweet, sweet cash, goes straight to home owners who make over six figures. Uncle Sam's giving money to rich people who can already afford homes. The story starts in 1913 when the government made all forms of interest tax deductible. But at that time, people who could buy homes bought them with cash. *Source: New York Times, Mar. 5, 2006. So homeowners didn't even have interest for them to deduct.*

But over the next few decades, the growth of credit cards led to a brand-new trend: debt and interest. And soon after, everybody was deducting everything.

But the government never intended this. So they closed that loophole in 1986. Except for mortgage interest. Congress was too scared to look like it was against the American dream of home ownership. So, even though we knew the tax break mainly helps the rich, we still have it for no good reason.

FUN FACT

BEFORE TOILET PAPER,
SOME AMERICANS USED CORNCOBS.

Source: Dugan, Bryan. "What Did People Use Before Toilet Paper?" Mental Floss. Dennis Publishing, 21 Feb. 2013. Web.

AIRBNB IS DANGEROUS FOR GUESTS AND HOMEOWNERS

Airbnb would have us believe it's a hospitality utopia, better than a hotel in every way. But the fact is, their business model and dangerous guests enables crooks, and could leave you on the hook for anything anyone does in your home.

The company doesn't even always insure homeowners.

In many cases, Airbnb has refused to pay for damages. One guest crammed a bunch of stuff down the owner's toilet, causing 10,000 dollars in damage. But Airbnb only offered to pay 78 dollars. *Source: Bort, Julie. "Airbnb Banned From Condo Complex After Guest Caused $10,000 Of Damage." Business Insider. Axel Springer SE, 9 Oct. 2014. Web.*

In another case, a guest refused to leave the property and became a squatter. After Airbnb wouldn't help, the host was forced to hire an expensive lawyer to evict them. *Source: Said, Carolyn. Squatters don't sit well with Airbnb hosts. San Francisco Chronicle. Hearst Corporation, 25 Jul. 2014. Web.*

The risk guests take is even worse. Hotels are required to undergo routine safety inspections, but no one checks Airbnb housing for working sprinklers, fire alarms, carbon monoxide detectors, or fire exists.

Airbnb will actually send a photographer to take pictures of your house, but they don't send anyone to make sure that it's safe.

In 2013, at least six Airbnb guests suffered carbon monoxide poisoning, and one of them died. We don't even know the total number of people who have been hurt by this incident because Airbnb refuses to release the numbers. *Source: Stone, Zak. "Living and Dying on Airbnb." Matter. Medium, 8 Nov. 2015. Web.*

Airbnb is particularly bad for cities. If landlords had their way, they would make every apartment a vacation rental.

So, to protect residents, cities pass laws that limit vacation rentals in apartment buildings. Problem is, Airbnb doesn't respect those laws. A 2014 report found that nearly three out of four Airbnb rentals in New York City were illegal. *Source: Streitfeld, David. "Airbnb Listings Mostly Illegal, New York State Contends." New York Times. The New York Times Company, 15 Oct. 2014. Web.*

ROY SAMAAN,

Research and Policy Analyst,
Los Angeles Alliance for a New Economy:

Roy Samaan: "Airbnb is used heavily by shady characters who use the service to run illegal hotel chains. They take out multiple leases in different buildings, and Airbnb those units year-round."

These jerks take critical residential housing out of the market, which drives up rent for all of us. And Airbnb does nothing to stop them. *Source: Monroe, Rachel. "More Guests, Empty Houses." Slate. Graham Holdings Company, 13 Feb. 2014. Web.*

Roy Samaan: "There was even a case in LA where a landlord evicted an entire apartment building so he could rent out the rooms on Airbnb. Left unregulated, Airbnb can destroy entire neighborhoods.

"Airbnb is a big tech company, and they can filter out illegal listings very easily. Instead, they're putting the burden on us and on cities

to go one-by-one and sue these landlords to make sure they're not breaking the law. And that just isn't fair."

Not only does Airbnb know about these crooks, they actually take a cut. If three out of four Craigslist users were using the site to commit murder, we'd be like, somebody stop that murder website.

Not only does Airbnb profit from illegal activity, they've even secretly purged the records of illegal listings from data they've released to make it look like it's not happening. *Source: Bromwich, Jonah. "Airbnb Purged New York Listings to Create a Rosier Portrait, Report Says." New York Times. The New York Times Company, 11 Feb. 2016. Web.*

It's a shame, because Airbnb actually provides a valuable service—especially in remote areas that don't have hotels. But they also need to be a good neighbor. Right now, they're doing the opposite.

Nobody wants to see people sleeping on the street, without a place to stay.

Oh, yeah, that reminds us...

EVERYTHING YOU KNOW ABOUT HOMELESSNESS IS WRONG

None of the things many homeless outreach centers do will accomplish an end to homelessness.

Feeding the homeless doesn't change the fact that they don't have homes. Not hot meals, substance abuse counseling, or job training.

Why would someone need to be sober before they can have a place to live?

Addiction is a disease. Can you imagine refusing someone housing for any other disease? Should diabetes prevent someone from getting a home?

Research shows programs that require abstinence place such a burden on the homeless that many drop out and return to living on the streets. *Source: Melbin, Anna. "Services Optional: Using a Voluntary Services Approach." National Alliance to End Homelessness. 8 Feb. 2012. Web.*

So what about job training? Giving the homeless skills so they can get a job and afford a home?

Even if you're trained, think about how hard it is to get a job if you don't have a place to live.

The services these places provide are well-intentioned and kind, but they're doing nothing to solve the real problem. *These people still don't have homes*.

IT'S NOT HOPELESS

There is a miraculously simple way to fix this, and it's being used to great effect all across the country.

Just give them homes.

And, yeah, that's a thing we can do.

RUDY SALINAS,

Program Director at Housing Works LA:

Rudy Salinas: "With Housing First, we prioritize putting people who experience chronic homelessness in their own permanent housing. Once we put a person in an apartment, we're able to address all the issues and causes why they became homeless in the first place. Studies have shown that when you put a person in their own permanent housing, their health improves significantly and you're able to effect change in their lives."

Not to mention that—once they have a home—they're no longer, you know, homeless. *Source: Santich, Kate. "Cost of homelessness in Central Florida? $31K per person." Orlando Sentinel. Tronc, Inc., 21 May 2014. Web.*

Rudy Salinas: "This is the new method being used across the country to address homelessness, and it's been proven to have great results."

In Utah, Housing First cut the number of chronically homeless by 90 percent in just ten years.

And it didn't cost a fortune.

It actually saved money.

When people live on the street, our taxes have to pay for their emergency services, law enforcement, and hospital visits. In Utah, the average yearly cost per homeless person was over 19,000 dollars. But the cost for giving someone a home and a counselor was just 7,800 dollars. That means Utah actually saved over 11,000 dollars for every person they gave a home to. *Source: Rascon, Jacob. "Utah's Strategy for the Homeless: Give Them Homes." NBC News. NBCUniversal, 3 May 2015. Web.*

It's counterintuitive, but let's put it this way: You can either let a person in need sleep on the street and waste money, or give them a home and save money.

MEET DOROTHY EDWARDS

She's one of Rudy's coworkers, and she used to be homeless.

Dorothy Edwards: "Yeah, I was homeless for fifteen years. I had no future, I had no hope, I was addicted to drugs, living in a tent on the side of the freeway. I was dying on the streets, literally dying. And then one day I was approached by Housing Works, and they said, you know, there's this Housing First model that's new, we'd like you to be a part of it. And they got me this great home that I live in today, look at this place.

"I've grown so much living there the last four years, it changed everything. I'm off of drugs, clean and sober. I became a homeless advocate myself. I speak on national and state levels for policy change."

Rudy Salinas: "The organization's practicing Housing First nationwide. You may wanna contact your local homeless service provider."

Ever wonder where the Hollywood sign came from? Well, it was actually an ad for a real estate development. It was built in 1923, and originally read "Hollywoodland." The idea for the sign came from investor Harry Chander.

Hollywoodland was a segregated housing plan built for white people who were trying to get away from Asian and Hispanic farm workers in the valley.

But the only thing stronger than systemic racism was the stock market crash of 1929.

The development never took off, and over the coming decades, the sign fell into disrepair. One time the "H" even fell over. Soon after, the sign was almost torn down. But get this: It was saved twice by none other than Hugh Hefner. Once in 1978, and again in 2010. *Source: Los Angeles Times, Apr. 27 2010.*

So the next time you see the Hollywood sign, remember, it's a big tacky billboard for a racist real estate plan propped by the king of porn. And there's nothing more Hollywood than that.

FINAL WORD

It's incredibly hard to find a place to live in America. Our housing system is a mess, and no one is talking about it.

Our country is in the middle of a housing crisis. Now, over half a million people in the U.S. are homeless. Homeowners are struggling to pay their mortgages, and nearly half of all renters are spending 30 percent of their income on rent.
Source: "Housing Challenges." The State of the Nation's Housing 2015. Cambridge: Joint Center for Housing Studies of Harvard University, 2015. 30-35. Web.

We need to eliminate our infatuation with home ownership, and build low-cost rentals.

Place common sense regulations on Airbnb and provide the chronically homeless with places to live. If we do all those things, we'll be that much closer to providing everyone with a comfortable, affordable home.

ADAM RUINS
DRUGS

DIRECTOR: J.J. ADLER

ORIGINAL AIR DATE: NOVEMBER 15, 2016

It's time to weed through the myths that surround marijuana, deal with the blunt truths about America's war on drugs, and show how prescription pills are the real gateway drug.

FOR MOST PEOPLE, WEED IS ESSENTIALLY HARMLESS

And we've known it for decades. Counting deaths from the substance alone, alcohol kills 88,000 people a year. Tobacco kills 480,000. And marijuana kills absolutely no one. *Sources: Shapiro, Maren.* *"No High Risk: Marijuana May be Less Harmful Than Alcohol, Tobacco." NBC News. NBCU-*

niversal, 26 Feb. 2015. Web. Centers for Disease Control and Prevention. "Smoking and To-bacco Use." Atlanta, 2016. Web. National Institutes of Health. National Institute on Alcohol Abuse and Alcoholism. "Alcohol Facts and Statistics." Washington, 2016. Web.

And, yeah, we know, that's not what they teach. Educators have been saying it's a gateway drug for years, but it's not true. Most people who try marijuana don't even continue smoking marijuana. *Source: U.S. Department of Health and Human Services. Substance Abuse and Mental Health Services Administration. "Results from the 2012 National Survey on Drug Use and Health: Summary of National Findings." Rockville, 2012. Web.*

Now, that doesn't mean that it's perfectly safe.

If you're under twenty-five, smoking weed can lead to memory problems and poor cognitive functioning. *Source: Fleming, Kelly. "What Smoking Weed Does to Teen Brains." The Stranger. Index Newspapers, LLC, 22 Oct. 2014. Web.* But if you're an adult and your brain has finished developing, it's really your choice.

The truth is, if you know the risks and you use it in moderation, weed is no big deal. And, in fact, humans have been using it for millennia. Humans started growing canna-bis as a crop over 8,000 years ago. *Source: Gray, Alic William et al. "Origins of Agriculture." Encyclopedia Britannica. Encyclopedia Britannica, Inc., 29 Sep. 2015. Web.*

In 440 BCE, Herodotus wrote about the ancient tradition of cannabis steam baths. *Source: Herodotus. The History of Herodotus. 440 B.C.E. Web.*

And in America, marijuana was available for many years in over-the-counter medications.

For most of America's history, weed was legal and no one cared about it.

So, what changed?

HERE'S THE WEIRD REASON WE BANNED WEED

Enter Harry Anslinger, the Commissioner of the Federal Bureau of Narcotics and a staunch prohibitionist.

His logic went something like this: The Federal Bureau of Narcotics had its funding cut circa 1930. He needed to demonize a new chemical to keep the funding flowing, and he needed to link it to something people were afraid of for no good reason. He settled on Mexicans. And Mexicans smoked marijuana. *Source: Booth, Martin. Cannabis: A History. New York: Thomas Dunne Books/St. Martin's Press, 2004. Web.*

...Yep. That's it.

Anslinger used that racism to fuel a propaganda campaign against the drug, testifying before Congress:

"Marijuana is an addictive drug, which produces in its users insanity, criminality and death." *Source: Booth, Martin. Cannabis: A History. New York: Thomas Dunne Books/St. Martin's Press, 2004. Web.*

Soon the "marijuana causes violence" meme was everywhere, from newspapers to movies.

Source: Backstory Radio. "All Hopped Up: Drugs in America." Virginia Foundation for the Humanities, 16 Aug. 2013. Web.

From *Reefer Madness*: "Just a young boy, under the influence of the drug, he killed his entire family with an axe."

To subtle political cartoons, like "The Marijuana Smoker." (As for why the racist caricature would be saying "Nazi propaganda," we have no idea.)

But it worked.

In 1937, Congress banned marijuana. And later, with Anslinger's help, they passed the first mandatory minimum sentencing laws, which made it so that your first time getting caught with this could put you away for two to ten years.

And the true irony is, the government knew Anslinger's claims were false.

Scientists proved marijuana wasn't connected to violence or insanity in the '40s. And in 1973, a bipartisan commission recommended Nixon decriminalize it. But Nixon, being Nixon...didn't. *Source: National Commission on Marihuana and Drug Abuse. "Marihuana: A Signal of Misunderstanding." 1973. Web.*

Nixon was not a man known for being chill.

In fact, in 1994, Nixon's aide—John Ehrlichman—said:

"We knew we couldn't make it illegal to be either against the war or black, but by getting the public to associate the hippies with marijuana and blacks with heroin, and then criminalizing both heavily, we could disrupt those communities. We could arrest their leaders, raid their homes, break up their meetings, and vilify them night after night on the evening news. Did we know we were lying about the drugs? Of course we did." *Source: Baum, Dan. "Legalize It All." Harper's Magazine. Harper's Magazine Foundation, Apr. 2016. Web.*

Nixon started the war on drugs to bully his political enemies and minorities. His own aide admitted it.

THINGS HAVEN'T GOTTEN ANY BETTER

Despite laws being loosened in a few states, mandatory minimums are still in effect all across the country, and marijuana still accounts for nearly half of all drug arrests. *Source: FBI 2014.* And, despite the fact that white and black people smoke at basically the same rate, black people are four times as likely to be arrested for marijuana. *Source: Urbina, Ian. "Blacks Are Singled Out for Marijuana Arrests, Federal Data Suggests." New York Times. New York Times Company, 3 Jun. 2013. Web.*

Look, we know for a fact that weed isn't dangerous, but we're still following racist old laws and throwing countless people of color in prison for no reason.

AND THE DARE PROGRAM SUCKS

The Drug Abuse Resistance Education (DARE) program was a massive failure with horrific consequences.

The "just say no" propaganda DARE advocates pedal can actually *increase* drug use.

This zero tolerance, abstinence only approach took off in the '80s, when Nancy Reagan said those three little words. *Source: Roe, Mike. "12 Videos from Nancy Reagan's 'Just Say No' Campaign." KPCC. National Public Radio, 7 Mar. 2016. Web.*

Soon, anti-drug messages were showing up in commercials, before arcade games, and even on TV shows.

In public schools, the bright, happy face of zero tolerance was DARE.

Study after study found that DARE had no effect on drug use at all. In fact, one major study found that, for some kids, it actually increased drug use...maybe because showing kids a briefcase full of drugs is a great way to cultivate a hobbyist interest in drug varieties. *Source: Rosenbaum, Dennis P. and Gordon S. Hanson. "Assessing the Effects of School-Based Drug Education: A Six-Year Multilevel Analysis of Project D.A.R.E." Journal of Research in Crime & Delinquency 35.4 (1998): 381-412. Web.*

At its peak, DARE cost U.S. taxpayers up to 1.3 billion dollars, even though it straight up did not work. *Source: Shepard, Edward M. "The Economic Costs of D.A.R.E." Institute of Industrial Relations, Nov. 2001. Web.*

AND THE GOVERNMENT KNEW IT DIDN'T WORK

Back in 1994, a government-funded study found that DARE did absolutely nothing. But then DARE pressured those behind the study into disavowing it. *Source: "Truth & DARE." Frontline. Public Broadcasting Station, 5 Mar. 1998. Web.*

The evidence is clear. The zero-tolerance approach does not work.

The war on drugs has been a massive failure. And the harsh enforcement tactics we've been using since the '80s have only made the drug problem worse. We've spent millions upon millions raiding outdoor marijuana farms.

But that's just made growers switch to hydroponic grow rooms, which help create a much stronger product. *Source: Pollan, Michael. The Botany of Desire: A Plant's Eye View of the World. New York: Random House, 2001. Web.*

AND THE WAR ON DRUGS DIDN'T MAKE DRUGS HARDER TO GET

Since the drug wars started, the prices of cannabis, cocaine, and even heroin, have all plummeted. *Source: Werb, Dan, et al. "The Temporal Relationship between Drug Supply Indicators: an Audit of International Government Surveillance Systems." BMJ Open 3.9 (2013). Web.*

They're not even locking up the bad guys.

We've locked up tons of non-violent drug offenders, but the vicious kingpins at the top are still making bank. The U.S. illicit drug market is worth an estimated 109 billion dollars a year, and the Sinaloa drug cartel has as many as 150,000 employees.

That's more than Apple. *Source: Keefe, Patrick Radden. "Cocaine Incorporated." New York Times Magazine. New York Times Company, 15 Jun. 2012. Web.*

SHERIFF JOHN URQUHART,

King County, Washington:

"You know, before I was sheriff, I was a narcotics detective, and I fought the war on drugs at the ground level. Now I've been in law enforcement for forty years, and it's become very obvious to me that the war on drugs hasn't worked. Now, over the last few decades, we've spent over one trillion dollars fighting the war on drugs, and this is how much drug use has dropped in America.

"Drug addiction is a health issue, but we've spent so much time locking people up that we've ignored that. We don't lock up people who need insulin shots, why should we lock up people for this disease? And the war on drugs has been an abject failure."

LEGAL DRUGS ARE EVEN WORSE THAN ILLEGAL ONES

Hate to break it to you, but some prescription drugs are almost identical to street drugs. Kids across America take the prescription drug Adderall, which is an amphetamine. You know what else is an amphetamine? Meth.

The chemical composition of the two drugs is nearly identical. And, in one study, people who took both couldn't even tell the difference. *Source: Kirkpatrick, Matthew G., et al. "Comparison of Intranasal Methamphetamine and D-amphetamine Self-Administration by Humans." Addiction 107.4 (2012): 783-791. Web.*

Now, Adderall still helps a lot of people. But the fact remains, we're giving kids essentially the same drug we make scary TV shows about.

And the line gets blurrier.

Heroin was first marketed and sold by the drug company, Bayer— you know, the Aspirin people. *Source: "Bayer AG." Encyclopedia Britannica. Encyclopedia Britannica Inc., 2016. Web.*

Anyone could just go into a store and buy heroin. They even gave it to kids. *Sources: Business Insider, Nov. 17 2011.*

Heroin was considered so safe, one medical journal even claimed that there was no danger of acquiring a habit. *Source: Boston Medical and Surgical Journal. Cupples, Upham & Company, 1900. Web.*

DOCTORS STILL PRESCRIBE DRUGS LIKE THIS

Heroin is an opioid, so when it was banned, scientists just invented new opioids that act on the exact same receptors in the brain. *Source: Anesthesiology, Dec. 2011.*

In the '90s, drug maker, Purdue, started marketing OxyContin like crazy, producing weird swag like plush toys, golf balls, and even a swing CD. And OxyContin's popularity soared. *Source: Quinones, Sam. Dreamland: The True Tale of America's Opiate Epidemic. New York: Bloomsbury Press, 2015. Web.*

This led to a surge in painkiller abuse and overdoses.

This was great for Purdue. By 2016, OxyContin alone had made them 31 billion dollars. *Source: LA Times, May 5, 2016.*

Purdue even issued an internal memo encouraging sales people to push higher doses in exchange for bonuses. *Source: Ryan, Harriet, Lisa Girion and Scott Glover. "'You Want a Description of Hell?': Oxycontin's 12-Hour Problem." Los Angeles Times. tronc Inc., 5 May 2016. Web.* And this disgusting greed caused a lot of harm. In 2014 alone, prescription opioids caused almost 19,000 overdose deaths, double the number from heroin.

Realizing there was a big problem, lawmakers made prescription opioids way harder to get.

This was...actually not good.

Thanks to the war on drugs, there was a ton of heroin in the streets, and it was really cheap. *Source: Centers for Disease Control and Prevention. "Today's Heroin Epidemic." Atlanta, 2016. Web.*

Source: Centers for Disease Control and Prevention. Division of Vital Statistics, Mortality Data. Atlanta, 2014. Web.

Since the government cracked down on painkillers, heroin deaths have skyrocketed. Between 2010 and 2015, they more than tripled—and some studies found that 80 percent of new heroin users got started on prescription opioids. *Source: Centers for Disease Control and Prevention. Division of Vital Statistics, Mortality Data. Atlanta, 2014. Web.*

And now people are getting hooked on something even worse: Fentanyl. It's a highly addictive prescription opioid that's up to fifty times stronger than heroin, and it's killing people like crazy. *Source: CNN, May 11, 2016.*

EVER WONDER WHY...

Ah, fish oil, the trendiest and stinkiest health fad of the moment.

Ever wonder why it gives you such gross burps?

Because most of it is rancid.

Fish oil is actually a delicate product that requires very careful processing to make sure the oil doesn't oxidize.

This oxidization occurs when fish oil comes into contact with heat, light, or oxygen. And if you've noticed, heat, light, and oxygen are...everywhere. So, oxidization happens all the dang time.

One study found that out of thirty-six fish oil products tested, over half had oxidized above the recommended limit. And, on average, only contains 68 percent of the omega three fatty acids that were listed on the label. *Source: NZ Herald, Jan. 22, 2015.*

So, what will happen if you eat this stinky fish juice? No one knows yet. *Source: Journal of Nutritional Science, Nov. 23, 2015.* But a good rule of thumb is, if it tastes bad, which this stuff definitely does, don't eat it. Leave the fish goop in the ocean where it belongs.

DON'T BE A DOPE

Look, for decades, our government told us that weed was a gate-way drug...while the real gateway drug was being legally prescribed by doctors all across America.

And because we ignored that fact, we now have a prescription drug epidemic and a heroin epidemic.

Here's the conundrum well-meaning people have: How do they get people to stop using illicit drugs?

Honestly? You can't.

Throughout human history, people have made drugs, other people have taken those drugs, and some of them have gotten addicted. Doing drugs is just something humans do. There's no way to stop it completely.

BUT WE CAN REDUCE THE HARM DRUGS CAUSE

Injection sites like Insight have operated across the world for de-cades, and in that time, there has not been a single death in any facility. *Source: Addiction, June, 2007.*

DONALD MACPHERSON,

Executive Director of the Canadian Drug Policy Coalition:

Donald MacPherson: "In Vancouver we learned that addiction is really a health issue, so we opened a health facility called Insight, where people can come and inject their drugs under medical supervision, without fear of arrest or of dying from an overdose."

Doesn't using drugs openly encourage drug use?

Donald MacPherson: "People are using these drugs whether we like it or not, and places like Insight prevents them from dying unnecessarily. On Thanksgiving weekend last year, 33 people overdosed at Insight on Fentanyl and none of them died because there were people there to help. Sadly, down the street, a young woman injected alone in a hotel room and she died. These deaths are preventable."

THE BOTTOM LINE

We need to accept that drug use is a fact of life. Instead of demonizing weed for no reason, pushing zero tolerance, or throwing drug addicts in jail, we should use harm reduction so we can actually help people and save lives.

How about this: Instead of "just say no," let's "just say, go research harm reduction strategies for your community."

EVER WONDER WHY...

Ever wonder why we put Q-tips in our ears? Because if you look at a box of Q-tips, they have an explicit instruction: *Warning, do not insert swab into ear canal.* That's right, Q-tips literally warns us not to use their product in the exact way everyone uses them. That's like if we were all eating those do not eat dehydration packs that came in beef jerky.

In fact, when Q-tips were invented, they weren't designed to be used in ears at all. When they came out in 1923, they were marketed as swabs for babies, and were known as "baby gays." *Source: Washington Post, Jan. 20 2016.*

And there's a very good reason that they tell us not to put Q-tips in our ears. When you swab your ear canal, you're actually pushing some ear wax deeper in, instead of taking it out. This can induce hearing loss and—if you push in too deeply—can even rupture your eardrum. *Source: WBUR, Nov. 28 2012.*

The fact is, we don't need to remove ear wax in the first place. We think wax is dirty, but it's necessary to protect your ears from dirt and, yes, even little bugs.

But when you use a Q-tip to remove wax from your ears, it leaves you vulnerable.

So, no matter how good it feels, please, listen to me and to the people who make the dang things, do not put Q-tips in your ears.

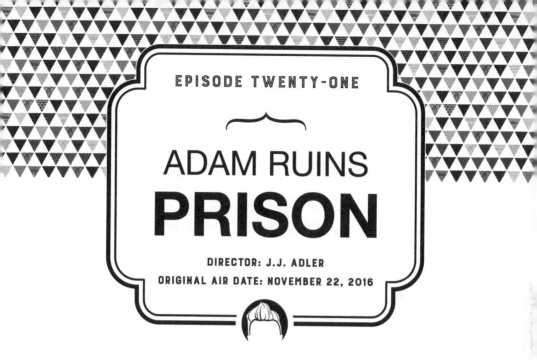

ADAM RUINS
PRISON

DIRECTOR: J.J. ADLER
ORIGINAL AIR DATE: NOVEMBER 22, 2016

The American prison system is completely screwed up. Which, given the episode guide you're currently reading, should come as no shock. Corporations make money off of inmates, the concept of jail rehabilitation is wrong, and solitary confinement is akin to torture.

THE PRISON SYSTEM IS A FAILURE ON EVERY LEVEL

Whatever purpose you think the American prison system serves, it ain't doing it.

It sure as heck isn't reducing crime, for one thing.

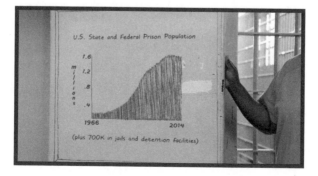

There are 2.2 million people incarcerated in the U.S., ten times more than fifty years ago. *Source: Report of The Sentencing Project to the United Nations Human Rights Committee: Regarding Racial Disparities in the United States Criminal Justice System. Washington: The Sentencing Project, 2013. Web.*

Two million is more than the population of some states.

But despite this massive increase in the prison population, a 2015 study conducted by the NYU School of Law found that the effect on the crime rate has been essentially zero.

SO WHY DO WE LOCK SO MANY PEOPLE UP?

Pretty often, it's to make money.

It all started in the tough-on-crime '80s, when the war on drugs meant state and federal prisons were bursting at the seams.

Governments decided to let corporate America handle their prisons.

And so, the Corrections Corporation of America (CCA), was born.

"OK, hold on," you might be thinking. "You can't just sell prisons like they're cars or real estate or hamburgers."

Well….

Tell that to Tom Beasley, the co-founder of CCA, who once said, "You just sell prisons like you were selling cars or real estate or hamburgers."

"YOU JUST SELL [PRISONS] LIKE YOU WERE SELLING CARS, OR REAL ESTATE, OR HAMBURGERS."

TOM BEASLEY, 1988

Source: Larson, Erik. "Captive Company." Inc. Mansuento Ventures, 1 Jun. 1988. Web.

And they rake in a ton of money. Last year, CCA took in 1.7 billion dollars. Source: 2015 CCA Annual Report. Nashville: Corrections Corporation of America, 2016. Web.

NONE OF THIS SAVES TAXPAYERS MONEY

The data shows that private prisons cost the taxpayers just as much as regular prisons. Source: Oppel, Richard A. "Private Prisons Found to Offer Little in Savings." New York Times. New York Times Company, 18 May 2011. Web.

Today, nearly one-fifth of federal prisoners are held in a for-profit facility.

And holy crow, do they like handing out infractions...which ain't a coincidence.

One study showed that private prisons dole out twice as many infractions as government prisons. Source: Mukherjee, Anita. "Impacts of Private Prison Contracting on Inmate Time Served and Recidivism." University of Wisconsin Madison School of Business, 10 Aug. 2016. Web.

These penalties can lengthen your sentence, which earns the company even more cash. The more people that are in prison, the more money they make.

That's why private prisons sneak occupancy clauses into their contracts, which actually requires states to keep prisons full.

In 2015, a private prison in Arizona didn't make their 97 percent capacity quota. So the state government had to pay them a 3 million dollar fine. *Source: Ortega, Bob. "Arizona prison oversight lacking for private facilities." The Arizona Republic. Gannett Company, 7 Aug. 2011. Web.*

Fines like that incentivize cash-strapped states to keep people in prison as long as possible.

Not all prisons are private prisons, but those that are don't exist to stop crime. They exist to make money.

EVER WONDER WHY...

Ever wonder why Americans eat so much cheese? It's everywhere. Tacos, burgers, even inside our pizza crust.

Well, it all started during the Great Depression. The dairy industry was on the brink of collapse.

So the government decided to bail them out. *Source: Smithsonian.com, Aug 31, 2016.*

For decades to come, America used tax dollars to buy up a whole bunch of cheese and save big cow.

The United States bought so much excess dairy, they needed somewhere to store it. So they made a...somewhat questionable choice.

The government found some caves in Missouri and packed them full of cheese and butter. By 1983, these literal "cheese caves" held over 4 billion dollars worth of dairy products. And they still exist to this day. *Source: New York Times, Nov. 6, 2010.*

The government had so much excess cheese, they gave it away to those in need. Also known as "government cheese."

And to this day, the government still provides money to fast food companies to help them market cheese-heavy products. *Source: Mother Jones, June 23, 2014.*

That's why America is wild about cheese.

SOLITARY CONFINEMENT IS A CRUEL AND INHUMANE PUNISHMENT THAT HAS NO PLACE IN MODERN SOCIETY

Solitary confinement has devastating effects on prisoners' mental health.

In solitary, you're kept alone for twenty-three hours a day in a room the size of a king-size bed. *Source: "Solitary Nation." Prod./Dir. Dan Edge. Frontline. Public Broadcasting Station, 22 Apr. 2014. Web.*

It's an archaic and cruel form of punishment that started in the 1800s.

Solitary confinement was conceived by Quakers, who thought prisoners would use the time to reflect and study the Bible. *Source: Casella, Jean and James Ridgeway. Hell is a Very Small Place: Voices from Solitary Confinement. New York: The New Press, 2016. Web.*

AS NOT SEEN ON TV ✂

Act II of this episode, about solitary confinement, was challenging to pull off. Not only is it such a serious topic, but it's difficult to make a tiny jail cell visually engaging enough to hold the audience's attention. Writer Diona Reasonover took special care to come up with visual elements that added interest, without being disrespectful or detracting from the overall tone. It was also important to the team that Kendra be the one to guide much of the episode, given the disproportionate impact mass incarceration has on people of color.

But even they decided it was too cruel to use. The Supreme Court at the time declared:

"Prisoners subject to solitary confinement became violently insane. Others committed suicide."

Solitary confinement fell out of use in the U.S. for a century. But a few decades ago we brought it back, and it's been destroying minds ever since.

Humans are social animals, meaning a prolonged lack of social contact can cause serious and permanent brain damage. People held in solitary confinement hallucinate, fall into depression, and lose the ability to keep track of how much time has passed. *Source: Gawande, Atul. "Hellhole." New Yorker. Conde Nast, 30 Mar. 2009. Web.*

SOLITARY ISN'T JUST FOR THE "WORST OF THE WORST"

Solitary confinement is routinely used in our prison system. It's basically given to anyone the guards don't want to deal with. *Source: "The Dangerous Overuse of Solitary Confinement in the United States." New York: American Civil Liberties Union, 2014. Web.*

Solitary confinement is given to between 80,000 and 100,000 people a year. *Source: The Guardian, Apr. 27, 2016.*

There are actually entire prisons made up of nothing but solitary cells. They're called supermax prisons. Enormous complexes full of people held in tiny cages like animals, slowly being driven insane.

They may be criminals, but they don't deserve this.

And it gets worse.

Research shows that solitary causes a syndrome called "delirium." People with delirium don't just hallucinate, they have difficulty thinking. They have panic attacks. And they suffer from overt paranoia. And once they're released from solitary, the outside world can be too much for them. *Source: Washington University Journal of Law and Policy, 2006.*

There was a teenager at Riker's named Kalief Browder. He was accused of stealing a backpack.

He was held in solitary for almost two years. And then his case was thrown out. He never even went to trial and still had to suffer through solitary. And when he got out, his family said that he would hole up in his room for days.

He committed suicide. *Source: Gonnerman, Jennifer. "Kalief Browder Learned How to Commit Suicide on Rikers." New Yorker. Conde Nast, 2 Jun. 2016. Web.*

Some prisoners are kept in solitary for decades. Decades. And then one day, shoved back into society. Often in worse mental shape than when they arrived.

Put all that together, and it's hard to escape the conclusion that solitary confinement should be considered a form of torture.

EVER WONDER WHY...

Ever wonder why treadmills are so un-fun? Even the name sounds grueling. Tread-mill. It turns out treadmills were actually invented as a form of punishment for prisoners.

In 1818, a British engineer named William Cubitt designed the first treadmill. The treadwheel, or "ever-lasting staircase," would often be used to grind grain or pump water. *Source: Encyclopedia Britannica, 2016.* And the target market for his new device was prisons.

Some prisoners would be made to climb for ten hours a day, up to 12,000 feet. *Source: Harvard University Library, Mar. 1, 2015.* That's about as high as the Empire State Building, every single day.

In the end, the treadmill as punishment was abandoned, because the practice was seen as too cruel. And now, we use it to torture ourselves at the gym. So next time you hop on, just be glad you'll be able to hop off whenever you want.

REHABILITATION IS NOW BORDERLINE IMPOSSIBLE

Rehabilitating folks should be the goal of our prison system. Too bad it actively does the opposite.

People are being set up to fail.

It's been years since the "prison education" fantasy was a reality.

Back in 1847, Sing Sing's prison education program had a curriculum that included reading, writing, math, history, geography, physiology, and even Phys. Ed. *Source: Messemer, Jonathan E.*

"The Historical Practice of Correctional Education in the United States: A Review of the Literature." International Journal of Humanities and Social Sciences 1.17 (2011): 91-100. Web.

But government budget cuts have systematically eliminated any opportunity for people to educate themselves while in prison.

In 1994, tough-on-crime was all the rage and American politicians hated the idea that prisoners should get anything.

Since then, we've gone from having 350 college degree programs for prisoners across the country, to just twelve. And good luck getting into the programs that do exist. The largest prison training program in the country has a waiting list of 10,000 people. *Source: Horwitz, Sari. "U.S. official says prison system's best reentry program cut 'dramatically.'" Washington Post. Nash Holdings LLC, 29 Oct. 2015. Web.*

And this is a real shame, because studies show that education is the easiest, cheapest way to reduce recidivism. Right now, 40 percent of federal prisoners are back behind bars within just three years.

And instead of trying to reduce that number, this system does everything in its power to make sure that we end up back there again.

DARYL ATKINSON, JD
Second Chance Fellow
U.S. DEPARTMENT OF JUSTICE

DARYL ATKINSON,

Lawyer, Second Chance Fellow, U.S. Justice Department:

Daryl Atkinson: "In 1996, I was convicted of a first-time, nonviolent drug crime and sentenced to ten years in prison. I did my time, got out, got my education, my law degree and now here I am."

He did all of this *after* prison.

Daryl Atkinson: "People who leave prison face a litany of barriers. Their rights are stripped away and it impacts every aspect of their daily lives. They have no money, but they have to pay for their own ankle monitors and other fees associated with their incarceration. *Source: Stillman, Sarah. Get Out of Jail, Inc. New Yorker. Conde Nast, 23 Jun. 2014. Web.* When they apply for a job, they have to check that box—'Have you ever been convicted of a felony?'—which immediately disqualifies them from even being considered. But finding a job is often a requirement of their parole.

"They can't find a place to live because they're discriminated against by landlords. They have no support for themselves or support from society. So it's no wonder that people keep coming back to prison. Instead of truly rehabilitating people, the system keeps setting them up to fail. America's supposed to be the land of second chances, but we continue to punish millions of American citizens again and again for things that they paid their debt to society for. It's just wrong." *Source: Childress, Sarah. "Michelle Alexander: 'A System of Racial and Social Control.'" PBS.org. Public Broadcasting Station, 29 Apr. 2014. Web.*

AND AMERICA'S RACE PROBLEM IS EVIDENT

Sixty percent of the prison population are people of color. Black men are six times more likely to be in prison than white men. *Source: "America's Disappeared Black Men." Washington: The Sentencing Project, 2015. Web. Whole communities are stuck in the cycle.*

Two million Americans are in prison. Two million are trapped in the system that profits off of them. They're shoved in tiny boxes where they go insane, and the system does everything it can to make sure they get locked up.

So, what's the point of prison?

Sure, seems like it's to get the people we're scared of as far away from us as possible...and then forget about them.

BUT WE CAN WORK TO CHANGE THE SYSTEM

If we really want to overhaul the system, we need to eliminate mandatory minimums and all of those harsh laws that turn people into second class citizens. And we need to ban solitary.

Those of us in positions of privilege should do something meaningful.

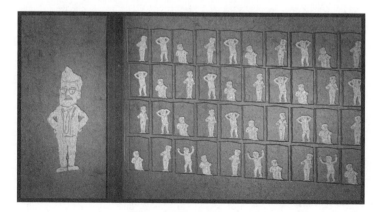

[Daryl Atkinson, left, with Dorsey Nunn]

DORSEY NUNN,

Executive Director of Legal Services for Prisoners with Children and Founder of All of Us or Nunn:

Dorsey Nunn: "Several decades after I got out of prison, I helped initiate a campaign called Ban the Box. The box is that question on applications, 'Have you ever been convicted of a felony?'" *Source: BanTheBoxCampaign.org, 2016.*

Daryl Atkinson: "And that box on this application, it puts formerly incarcerated people in a no-win situation. Either they have to lie and say they've never been convicted of a crime, or they check that box, face discrimination, and never get callbacks for interviews or jobs."

Dorsey Nunn: "We're not asking companies to hire people just because they've been to prison. We're asking for a fair chance to return to the community and actually be an asset instead of a liability."

Daryl Atkinson: "This is a campaign that helps our entire community by reducing recidivism and keeping our neighborhoods safe, something that everyone should be on board with."

EPISODE TWENTY-TWO

ADAM RUINS THE
WILD WEST

DIRECTOR: MATTHEW POLLOCK
ORIGINAL AIR DATE: NOVEMBER 29, 2016

The good, the bad and the...ruined. Saddle up as we explain how prostitutes actually helped settle the West, why the all-American cowboy is a myth, and who (or what) was the real hero of the West.

Yee-haw!

THE HEROIC COWBOY MYTH IS A CROCK OF CRAP

AS NOT SEEN ON TV ✂

The set locations provided by Los Angeles surrounding desert was a major reason that Westerns took off in the '50s. In keeping with that tradition, much of this episode was filmed near Joshua Tree National Park.

When we think of cowboys, we're usually thinking of a composite of Hollywood tropes. But the movie version of the Wild West had nothing to do with the real history.

Not even the clothing was right.

This is a more accurate cowboy appearance:

And he would've been a stinky fella.

That's because real cowboys didn't shoot bad guys—they herded cows. *Source: "The Last Cowboy," PBS.org, 2015.* They were basically just laborers.

COWBOYS WEREN'T THE LAW

The law was the law in Wild West towns, and many of them actually had stricter gun laws than those same cities today.

Frontier towns were industrial economies where people came to mine or herd cattle. So, many of them required visitors to check their firearms upon entering. *Source: Drogin, Bob. "Gun laws were tougher in old Tombstone." Los Angeles Times. tronc Inc., 23 Jan. 2011. Web.*

Source: Winkler, Adam. "Did the Wild West Have More Gun Control Than We Do Today?" The Huffington Post. AOL, 9 Sep. 2011. Web.

And cowboys were, very literally, *not* the "white knights" of the West.

Most cowboys weren't white at all. A third were Mexican, and a quarter were black. *Source: Haeber, Jonathan. "Vaqueros: The First Cowboys of the Open Range." National Geographic. National Geographic Society, 15 Aug. 2003. Web. Source: Ponsford, Matthew. "America's black cowboys fight for their place in history." CNN. Turner Broadcasting System, 28 Nov. 2012. Web.*

D. H. FIGUEREDO
Author - Revolvers and Pistolas, Vaqueros and Caballeros: Debunking the Old West

D. H. FIGUEREDO,
Author and Chronicler of the History of Mexicans in the West:

D. H. Figueredo: "The truth is that America owes most of its cowboy traditions to Mexican culture. Spain introduced cattle to Mexico in the 1500s. That's when the vaquero, or 'cow man,' was born."

That's why so many cowboy words derive from Spanish: lasso, rodeo, mustang, bronco, even chaps. *Source: "How We Know The American Cowboy Is A Latino Invention." The Huffington Post. AOL, 12 Dec. 2013. Web.*

D. H. Figueredo: "After the rise of the movie industry, American popular culture was dominated by the image of the white and tall cowboy, because actors like John Wayne and Gary Cooper were the ones cast to play cowboys in the movies. So, the long history of the black and Latino cowboys was forgotten."

WHAT ABOUT "REAL" COW-BOYS LIKE WYATT EARP AND BUFFALO BILL?

Wyatt Earp was a con artist drifter who sold his story to Hollywood. And Buffalo Bill was an entertainer known for his tall tales. *Source: American Experience, Jan. 25, 2010.* See, for many years, Americans thought of Wild West settlements as trashy places. But Buffalo Bill changed all that with his touring Wild West shows. *Source: "New Perspectives on the West: William F. Cody." PBS.org. Public Broadcasting Station, 2001. Web.*

It was a circus show with a simple storyline. But, as it toured the country, it popularized the image of the Wild West as we know it today. But that's all it was: a simple story.

COWBOYS DIDN'T FIGHT NATIVE AMERICANS

Nah. The American government did. *Source: "New Perspectives on the West." PBS.org, 2001.*

For centuries, the U.S. government systematically forced native people off their land, gave it to white homesteaders, and then, either killed the natives or confined them to reservations.

We didn't need protecting from Native Americans—they needed protecting from us. Our government straight-up invaded their home.

Americans have known about this for over a century. But instead of confronting it, we're still propagating a false image of the Wild West we got from a one-hundred-year-old circus act.

Ever wonder why Johnny Appleseed planted all those seeds? Most people assume that Johnny Appleseed just really, really loved apples.

But John Chapman, a.k.a. Johnny Appleseed, didn't do it for the love of apples. He did it for the love of cash.

In some parts of the country, if you planted enough seeds, you could claim the land as your own.

So, he went ahead of the settlers and planted a bunch of trees, and then sold all the land he claimed. *Source: Smithsonian.com, Nov. 10, 2014.*

And these apples weren't even apples you can eat—they were smaller, and much more tart. They were called "spitters." Not great for eating, but perfect for boozing.

Folks back then fermented spitters into cider. And since water wasn't safe to drink at the time, everyone just got buzzed on cider 24/7. *Source: Pollan, Michael, The Botany of Desire, Ch.1.*

So, the next time someone tells you Johnny Appleseed was a hero, tell them they're right, because he performed the most heroic task of all: He kept America drunk.

AND THE WEST SURE AS HECK WASN'T SETTLED BY A GUY WITH A GUN

In fact, Old West towns were largely built by women.

FUN FACT

SARSAPARILLAS ARE GOOD FOR PSORIASIS.

Source: Thurmon, Francis M. "The treatment of psoriasis with a sarsaparilla compound." New England Journal of Medicine 227.4 (1942): 128-133.

Women arguably did more to develop the West than men did.

Women, like everyone else, came to the west for economic opportunity. And, despite its considerable downsides, prostitution was often the most lucrative line of work available to them.

In fact, before these women arrived, Wild West towns weren't really towns at all—they were more like work camps.

The men were so desperate for women, they would pay just to see a pair of women's undergarments. *Source: MacKell Collins, Jan. "Soiled Doves." True West Magazine. 30 Sep. 2013. Web.*

So when women came west, they saw a clear economic need.

Their services were in such demand, many of these women made more money than the men they served. And entire towns sprung up around brothels. It was the influx of women that finally turned these barren camps into bustling towns. *Source: Armitage, Susan H. "Revisiting 'The Gentle Tamers Revisited': The Problems and Possibilities of Western Women's History: An Introduction." Pacific Historical Review 61.4 (1992): 459-462.*

And, with all that wealth, they soon became leaders of their communities.

They used that power to provide services the West desperately need-ed. Madam Millie of New Mexico used her wealth to put local children through college. *Source: Birchell, Donna Blake. Wicked Women of New Mexico. Charles-ton: The History Press, 2014. Web.*

Colorado Madam, Laura Evans, provided workers' compensation for injured men, and sheltered victims of domestic abuse. *Source: Shovald, Arlene. "Learn the inside story of Laura Evans, local madam." The Harold Democrat. New Media Investment Group, 24 Jun. 2015. Web.*

Madam "Diamond" Jessie Hayman provided food and clothing to the homeless after the 1906 San Francisco earthquake. *Source: Russell, Thad-deus. A Renegade History of the United States. New York: Free Press, 2011. Web.*

JAN MACKELL COLLINS
Author & Historian

JAN MACKELL COLLINS,
Author and Historian:

"So, it is true that the prostitution industry could be a very dangerous one, because there was disease, domestic vio-lence, drug abuse. But prostitutes were pioneers, just like the men they served. In fact, a lot of prostitutes and mad-ams were astute businesswomen. Being a prostitute or a madam could actually give women more financial freedom here in the West than their eastern counterparts, and that could even lead to a measure of political equality and influ-ence in the communities where they served these men."

By 1869, women wielded so much power in the West that Wyoming actually became the first territory to give women the right to vote, a half-century before the rest of the nation did. *Source: National-geographic.org, Jan. 21, 2011.*

Wyoming actually refused to become a state unless women kept that right.

"We may stay out of the Union 100 years, but we will come in with our women."
Wyoming Legislature

Source: Morrison, Patt. Lynne Cheney's Wild, Wild West. Los Angeles Times. tronc Inc., 11 Aug. 2004. Web.

Wyoming joined the Union as the Equality State, and the idea soon spread. The next eight states to grant women suffrage were all in the West. And Wyoming would go on to elect the nation's first female governor in 1924. Face it, without these women, the West as we know it wouldn't exist. *Source: "Women's Suffrage: Why the West First?" National Endowment for the Humanities, 2016. Web.*

Ah, the Statue of Liberty, an icon of Americana and a gift from France.

But ever wonder why it looks the way it does?

The statue, officially called Liberty Enlightening the World, was designed by Frederic Bartholdi, a Frenchman with a dream. *Source: Bereson, Edward. The Statue of Liberty: A Transatlantic Journey, Ch. 1.*

And the woman in the statue...was an Arab peasant woman.

Here's how it happened: Originally, Bartholdi tried to sell Egypt's ruler on a very similar design for the Suez Canal. *Source: The Daily Beast, Nov. 17, 2015.*

But Egypt wasn't having it. So, he decided to pitch his plan somewhere else.

Eventually, they decided on the final design for the statue, and that Egyptian peasant became the personification of American liberty.

So the next time you see it, remember, the Statue of Liberty—like most people in America—originally came here from another country.

THE REAL HERO OF THE WEST WASN'T A PERSON AT ALL

Frankly, the West probably never should have been settled at all. And, until surprisingly recently, very few people lived in these deserts.

Arizona, Nevada, and New Mexico are harsh, barren places with no water, and temperatures that regularly reach 110 degrees. People really only moved out West to work. And once that work dried up, they kept moving to more hospitable land.

Homesteaders who were given land in the Mojave Desert quickly abandoned their properties, and these places all became ghost towns. *Source: Martin, Hugo. "Tug of Wear Over Desert Homestead Shanties." Los Angeles Times. tronc Inc., 1 Nov. 2004. Web.* So, cowboys aren't the reason why modern Americans live out West. The only reason most people live there today is because of revolutionary modern technology.

To live here, we pipe cold air and water into this unlivable wasteland in defiance of God himself.

Air conditioning. Air conditioning won the war for the West.

We use vast amounts of energy to artificially terraform this desert wasteland, and it's all thanks to the federal government.

If you want to bring water and power to your inhospitable desert, try the Hoover Dam. A massive federal spending project built in 1935, it was the tallest dam in the world at the time, and it can be yours for nearly 800 million in today's dollars.

Between 1950 and 2000, Arizona's population quintupled, and Nevada's exploded by almost 1,000 percent. *Source: Lang, Robert E., and Kristopher M. Rengert. "The hot and cold sunbelts: Comparing state growth rates, 1950-2000." Fannie Mae Foundation (2001). Web.* Isn't the hubris of man beautiful?

So, remember, while tough guys want you to think that they did it themselves, the West—as we know it—was brought to you by modern technology and massive federal spending.

SPEAKING OF AIR CONDITIONING...

One of the reasons movie theaters first took off was they were the first public buildings to regularly feature AC.

This brought a huge influx of cash to the movie industry. And since then a new gold rush, opportunists like "hero" Wyatt Earp, went to Hollywood to peddle their tall tales.

Buffalo Bill's rodeo shows had whetted the public's appetite for frontier fiction. From the silent movie era through the '50s, one out of every five movies made was a western. It was these films that finally solidified the image of the lone, rugged cowboy we know today. *Source: Schatz, Thomas. "Cowboy Business." New York Times Magazine. The New York Times Company, 10 Nov. 2007. Web.*

SO, IN A NUTSHELL...

The modern West was settled by air conditioning. Air conditioning gave birth to the movie industry, and movies created the myth that cowboys settled the West.

Isn't it cool how it comes around like that? Man, history is so poetic sometimes.

COWBOYS ARE FETISHIZED, AND IT NEEDS TO STOP

The modern image of cowboys is part of a tale. And what a fascinating tale it is.

Black and Mexican cowboys, female governors, a cool air conditioner with a cowboy hat. Not to mention the rich history of the Native Americans which, frankly, deserves its own episode.

The true history is always more interesting than the myth.

It's time to let this fake story die and start telling the real one.

EPISODE TWENTY-THREE

ADAM RUINS THE
INTERNET

DIRECTOR: MATTHEW POLLOCK
ORIGINAL AIR DATE: DECEMBER 6, 2016

Guess what? Smartphones aren't really society-killers, Americans pay big for the worst internet speed in the world, and "free" sites are actually way costly. Let's surf the truthy highway.

THE INTERNET ISN'T RUINING SOCIETY

Every time technology advances, people say it's the end of the world. After the telephone was invented, newspapers worried it was so addictive we'd become a race of left-eared people. *Source: "Left-Earedness and the Telephone." New York Times. The New York Times Company, 20 Apr. 1904. Web.*

Concerns about smartphones being invasive with constant updates are also overblown. People said the same thing about another disturbingly fast modern device: the telegraph.

Newspapers got the same dang rap when they were invented. They were demonized for the exact same reasons. *Source: WNYC. Feb. 19, 2010.*

And before you get on the whole "nobody reads anymore" thing, more Americans read books today than did in the '50s. *Source: Madrigal, Alexis C. "The Next Time Someone Says the Internet Killed Reading Books, Show Them This Chart." The Atlantic. Atlantic Media Company, 6 Apr. 2012. Web.*

And, by the way, when books were invented, snobs hated on them, too. One intellectual even thought that too many books would harm the mind.

"...confusing and harmful abundance of books."
Conrad Gessner, 16th Century

Source: Nowak, Peter. "Boo! A brief history of technology scares." Maclean's. Rogers Media, 1 Nov. 2011. Web.

Socrates himself wasn't a big fan. The father of philosophy complained about the ultimate corrupting modern invention: the written word. *Source: Nowak, Peter. "Boo! A brief history of technology scares." Maclean's. Rogers Media, 1 Nov. 2011. Web.*

THINGS AREN'T WORSE NOW

"No, no, things are worse now. I can prove it. People used to communicate with each other, not like these solipsists."

Oh, hush.

The internet, and all of our smart devices, are literally used for communicating.

In fact, we're all communicating more now than we ever were before. We weren't better people back before we had smartphones or the internet, we were the same lazy, curious, social people we've always been. The only difference is now we have instantaneous access to all knowledge and communication. How is that anything other than a tremendous social good? Instead of pining for an imagined past, we should feel immensely lucky to live in the magnificent present.

Admit it. You love the internet.

Which is a shame. Because, as Americans, we pay a lot for some of the worst internet access in the modern world.

EVER WONDER WHY...

Ever wonder why people literally always misuse the word "literally"? The word literally means in a literal manner or sense. But people often use it to exaggerate for effect, and this drives some people nuts.

But, sorry, grammar nuts, this usage is not as wrong as you think. People have been using the word literally to mean figuratively for literally hundreds of years.

In fact, some of the English language's greatest writers used it that way. Mark Twain himself wrote that Tom Sawyer was "literally rolling in wealth." *Source: Twain, Mark. The Adventures of Tom Sawyer, Ch. 2.*

And Scott Fitzgerald wrote that Jay Gatsby "literally glowed." *Source: Fitzgerald, F. Scott. The Great Gatsby, Ch. 5.*

And don't forget Vladimir Nobakov, who wrote, "his eyes literally scoured the corners of his cell." *Source: Nobakov, Vladimir. Invitation to a Beheading. Ch. 3.*

Try as we might to resist, the fact is that words change and contain multiple meanings. "Literally" is just another example of that.

AMERICA'S INTERNET SUCKS

We actually have slower broadband than almost any other developed nation.

The internet in Seoul is nearly eight times faster than in America. *Source: PBS.org, Apr. 26, 2015.*

Cities in Korea, Japan, Switzerland, France, and even Romania, have internet fast enough to download an entire high definition movie in just seven seconds. *Source: Miller, Claire Cain. "Why the U.S. Has Fallen Behind in Internet Speed and Affordability." New York Times. The New York Times Company, 30 Oct. 2014. Web.*

And it ain't expensive. They pay as low as one-tenth of what many Americans pay. *Source: Russo, Nick et al. "The Cost of Connectivity 2014." New America Foundation, 2014. Web.* We are literally paying ten times as much for a fraction of the speed.

How is this possible?

Because the most hated companies in America are working to keep it that way.

Yeah, America's cable companies suck. They're monopolies. And they were created by local governments.

In exchange for building new cable lines, early cable companies were handed exclusive contracts by state and local governments. *Source: Honan, Mat. "Why the Government Won't Protect You from Getting Screwed by Your Cable Company." Gizmodo. Univision Communications, 15 Aug. 2011. Web.*

Those cable lines would go on to become the only viable way to get broadband to your home, so now if you want fast internet, you probably have no choice.

So, why don't other companies just put up new cables and try to compete?

That's the real scam: They all agreed not to. Years ago, America's cable companies realized that if they clustered themselves by region, they wouldn't really have to compete.

They hatched their plan in 1997, during what one cable executive called the "Summer of Love." *Source: Crawford, Susan P. "The Communications Crisis in America." Harvard Law and Policy Review. 5 (2011). Web.*

By 2016, America's forty regional cable companies had consolidated to just three, and without regional competition, they are free to jack up prices and keep your speeds shockingly slow. *Source: Vanity Fair. May 7, 2016.*

In other countries, service providers compete. In fact, France requires companies to share space on their networks with competitors, which is why some French people have not one—but six—high speed providers to choose from. *Source: Holmes, Allan and Zubak-Skees, Chris. "These maps show why internet is way more expensive in the US than Europe." The Verge. Vox Media, 1 Apr. 2015. Web.*

But in our country, these cable jerks have used every tool at their disposal to eradicate competition. They've even lobbied state governments to make it illegal for America's cities to build their own networks. *Source: Brodkin, Jon. "ISP lobby has already won limits on public broadband in 20 states." Ars Technica. Conde Nast, 12 Feb. 2012. Web.*

And this scheme makes the internet worse for all of us.

SUSAN CRAWFORD,

Professor, Harvard Law School:

Susan Crawford: "We think of ourselves as the most technologically advanced nation in the world, but when it comes to high speed internet access, we're at best in the middle of the pack.

"Look, the problem is that these very few companies are controlling Americans' access to the internet, and that means that everyday Americans are paying too much for second-class service. At a time when modern day life requires access to the internet, it's just as important these days as electricity or water."

The internet is essential to modern life.

Susan Crawford: "Exactly the same thing happened with electricity about one hundred years ago. It used to be considered a luxury, not a utility. And very few private companies controlled electricity in America. It took government intervention to make sure that all Americans had electricity."

Uncle Sam needs to do his job and force the cable companies to compete. Until he does, we're gonna keep getting screwed.

Susan Crawford: "If we don't upgrade the entire country to fiber optic internet access, we will be behind for the next several decades."

EVER WONDER WHY...

Ever wonder why the standard paper size is 8.5 x 11? Who decided that exact shape and size? It must have been the most boring man in the world. Well, not quite. It was one of our most boring presidents: Herbert Hoover.

In 1921, as Secretary of Commerce, the future president's snooze fest set up the Committee on the Simplification of Paper Sizes...and the rest is a snoozefest. *Source: The Law in Life, Sep. 22, 2013.*

Somehow, a heated debate broke out over what standards of paper sizes the government should use. People fell into one of two camps: 8.5 x 11, or 8 x 10.5.

Finally, after a lot of boring argument that we swear is not worth getting into, the 8 x 10.5s won. And that remained the standard paper size until 1980, when copiers became increasingly popular. *Source: Lawrence Journal-World, Jan. 13, 1979.*

So, the government went back to the drawing board because...maybe there nothing better was going on.

And that's how 8.5 x 11 became the standard paper size. We know you didn't ask—but hey—now you know.

NOT EVEN THE "FREE" STUFF ONLINE IS REALLY FREE

The truth is, "free" services like Google or Facebook aren't free at all. You pay for them with your very identity.

When you use Facebook, they log everything you do, the pages you like, the people you interact with, even the words in your status updates. Then they take information, analyze it, and assemble a detailed profile of who you are.

They know your habits, your preferences, they can even determine your risk tolerance or sexual orientation. *Source: The Guardian, Mar. 11, 2013.* And then they sell that information to advertisers. *Source: PNAS. Jan. 12, 2015.*

Say an advertiser wants to advertise to a risk-taking homosexual.... Well....

That's not hypothetical. This actually happened to a woman in Tampa. *Source: Angwin, Julia. Dragnet Nation: A Quest for Privacy, Security, and Freedom in a World of Relentless Surveillance. New York: Times Books, 2014. Web.*

People don't realize how deep Facebook's tentacles really go. They actually record which ads we see, then partner with firms that monitor what we do in the real world. *Source: Manjoo, Farhad. "Facebook Followed You to the Supermarket." Slate. Graham Holdings Company, 20 Mar. 2013. Web.*

This has gotta be one of the most invasive advertising systems ever devised. Facebook can actually determine who's the most vulnerable to an ad campaign, then up their dosage till they buy even more.

GOOGLE IS EVIL TOO

Google doesn't just track you when you search, their tracking software is also installed on over ten million websites—even medical sites. *Source: Empson, Rip. "Google Biz Chief: Over 10M Websites Now Using Google Analytics." TechCrunch. AOL, 12 Apr. 2012. Web.* So, that health info you think you're looking up in private, Google's got a front row seat.

And that's not all. Every time you compose an email through Gmail, watch a YouTube video, or use Google Maps, Google collects data about you. *Source: Peterson, Andrea. "How to make Google forget your most embarrassing searches." Washington Post. Graham Holdings Company, 5 Jul. 2016. Web.*

We don't even know the full extent of what Facebook and Google store, or what they do with it. All we know is that they're collecting our data on an unprecedented scale and making billions off of it. That's their real business model: They're monetizing us. When we use these sites, we're not the customer—we're the product.

ETHAN ZUCKERMAN,
Director of the MIT Center for Civic Media:

Ethan Zuckerman: "The fact that the sites are free is the problem. When the web was created we, the users, decided we would rather have free stuff than pay money for the services we used. As a result, the websites then had to sell ads to make money. They target ads to us based on our preferences and our behavior online, and that means we're under constant surveillance in exchange for these services that we get 'for free.'"

One in six people on Earth now has a Facebook account, and they make up 20 percent of all time spent online. *Source: D'Onfro, Jillian. "Here's how much time people spend on Facebook per day." Business Insider. Axel Springer SE, 8 Jul. 2015. Web.*

Ethan Zuckerman: "That's 1.6 billion people whose every move is being tracked by an online Big Brother that they chose to live under."

And here's the kicker: You wanna know how much revenue your personal data is worth to Facebook? For every user they surveil, they make just twelve dollars. Your interests, your personality, your relationships, your privacy, those things are priceless—but you gave them all away just to avoid paying twelve dollars.

THERE'S A WAY TO SAVE THE INTERNET

And we can all do it together by using the power of the internet itself.

In 2015, the cable companies were trying to do away with net neutrality—that's the principle that all data on the internet is treated equally. But instead of net neutrality, they wanted a system where rich sites could pay for faster service, while sites without money would get screwed.

Awful, right?

Susan Crawford: "That's what a lot of other people thought, too. But instead of staying silent, they used the internet to communicate with the FCC and their politicians and raised their voices. More than four million Americans wrote in to protect the internet they love. And, as a result of all that political pressure, the FCC changed direction. All those people made that happen. When you act collectively to ensure the protection of the internet, things change."

AS NOT SEEN ON TV ✂

The principle of net neutrality is still under constant threat in the United States, which would greatly increase the amount of power that cable companies with near-monopoly power already command. Please, keep tabs on the state of net neutrality over the coming years, and urge your representatives to defend it!

Ethan Zuckerman: "And we can do the same with Facebook and Google. We can demand more accountability for what these sites do with our data. And we can vote with our dollars by paying for sites that put our interests first."

Instead of being ashamed or scared of the internet, we should use the internet to raise our voices and fight for a better one.

We can all be superheroes.

ADAM RUINS
JUSTICE

DIRECTOR: TIM WILKIME
ORIGINAL AIR DATE: DECEMBER 13, 2016

It very often feels like it's just us in the justice system. And there are terrible reasons for that. In this episode, we'll reveal the struggles public defenders face, how juries are never completely impartial, and how everything you heard about the McDonald's coffee lady was wrong. Now, let's bang the gavel and get on with it.

THE MCDONALD'S HOT COFFEE LAWSUIT

This consumer suit was horrible, but not for the reasons you might think.

This was the public narrative: There was a greedy old lady. She gets a coffee at McDonald's but she's too dumb to know coffee is hot. Then she was driving like a crazy person and spilled a little in her lap. She decided to sue McDonald's because she thought she deserved money for being stupid and now she's a millionaire.

Well, all of that is wrong.

Here's what actually happened: Stella Liebeck was a seventy-

nine-year-old woman whose grandson drove her to McDonald's. She was in a parked car holding hot coffee in her lap when it spilled. Now, Stella openly admitted that the spill was her mistake, but the results were horrifying. She had third degree burns on her legs and genitals, and she went into shock. She had to undergo painful skin graft operations, and the surgeon said it was one of the worst cases he had ever seen. Stella was permanently disfigured and nearly died. *Source: Keneally, Meghan. "The truth behind the 'hot coffee' lawsuit: The elderly woman who became a punchline had 16% of her body covered in burns and McDonalds had ignored 700 earlier complaints about excessively hot drinks." The Daily Mail. DMG Media, 21 Oct. 2013. Web.*

The reason Stella's injuries were so severe is that McDonald's was serving coffee at up to 190 degrees. That's almost boiling. McDonald's even admitted that at that temperature, their coffee was a hazard. *Source: Haltom, William and Michael McCann. Distorting the Law: Politics, Media and the Litigation Crisis. Chicago: University of Chicago Press, 2004.* In fact, in the decade prior, over 700 people notified McDonald's that they'd been burned by their coffee.

The real irony is Stella didn't even wanna go to court, she just wanted McDonald's to help pay her 20,000 dollars in out-of-pocket medical expenses. But, after making her wait for six months, they only offered her 800 dollars.

Stella tried to get McDonald's to settle, she even agreed to mediation, but McDonald's wouldn't budge. They gave her no choice but to go to court. So, when the jury heard Stella's story, they found that McDonald's had acted so irresponsibly that they had to be punished.

And it worked.

In the end, Stella settled for less than 600,000 dollars, but that was enough to get McDonald's to lower their temperature and stop burning people. *Source: Cain, Kevin G. "And Now, the Rest of the Story... About the McDonalds Hot Coffee Lawsuit." The Houston Lawyer, Jul./Aug. 2007. Web.* This was an incredibly rare case where a working-class victim actually beat a huge team of corporate lawyers and made the world a better place.

WHY DOESN'T EVERYONE KNOW THIS?

Because those corporate lawyers are really good at their jobs.

They spent years running a disinformation campaign to convince Americans that there was an epidemic of frivolous lawsuits, and the media bought it.

And because of this false narrative, the witch hunt against frivolous lawsuits continues to this day.

Except it's largely a charade.

These protests have been organized and sponsored by large corporations.

MICHAEL MCCANN,

**Professor of Law and Politics
at the University of Washington,
Co-author of *Distorting the Law*:**

Michael McCann: "For the last several decades, with large corporations afraid of being seen for making unsafe products, created front groups like Citizens Against Lawsuit Abuse, try and turn public opinion against lawsuits. This included companies like Pfizer, Texaco, and big tobacco companies like Philip Morris." *Source: Deal, Carl and Joanne Doroshow. The CALA Files — The Secret Campaign by Big Tobacco and Other Major Industries to Take Away Your Rights. New York: New York Law School, 1999. Web.*

And by spreading this false story, they got everyone to believe that silly lawsuits were rampant.

Michael McCann: "But nothing could be further from the truth. The best social science evidence shows that the number of personal injury lawsuits in recent decades has declined, and the median payout is only 55,000 dollars." *Source: Cohen, Thomas H. Tort Bench and Jury Trials in State Courts, 2005. Washington: U.S. Department of Justice, 2009. Web.*

In short, these companies dragged an old lady through the mud so that we wouldn't be able to sue them anymore.

This story is insane. McDonald's had a policy that almost killed someone and it took Stella's lawsuit to change it. She should be considered a hero, but because of these companies, we treat her like a punchline.

Ever wonder why some people have photographic memories? Well, memorize this: Photographic memories don't exist. *Source: Scientific American, Jan. 1, 2013.*

Many people believe that there are folks out there whose minds can perfectly remember a mental snapshot. But when scientists actually test those people, they always come up short. Even though savants, whose brains come close, still mess up.

In 1970, a Harvard professor published a breakthrough study that seemed to prove his student had a photographic memory. He showed her a random pattern of 10,000 dots to one eye. And then a day later, showed another pattern of dots to her other eye. He claimed she was able to recall the separate patterns and fuse them in her mind to create a 3D image.

Isn't that amazing?

Except the professor then married his subject. She refused to be tested again, which made the study majorly suspect. *Source: Slate, Apr. 27, 2006.* So, how can we explain incredible feats of memory like people who can memorize entire books? One explanation is that these people have just mastered mnemonic techniques. It's impressive, but it's not photographic.

The truth is, there is no concrete evidence that anyone has a photographic memory.

THE JURY SYSTEM IS RIFE WITH BIAS

Trial by jury is the cornerstone of our democracy's legal system. In America, your fate isn't decided by a dictator or a king. Instead, justice is served by a jury of peers—your fellow citizens.

Thing is, if they're just like us, then they're gonna make a lot of mistakes. It is a testament to democracy, that our justice system gives such awesome power to average citizens...but that also means our juries are subject to the same biases we carry with us in everyday life.

One study did find that juries recommend more lenient sentences to attractive defendants. *Source: Gunnell, Justin J., and Stephen J. Ceci. "When Emotionality Trumps Reason: A Study of Individual Processing Style and Juror Bias." Behavioral Sciences & the Law 28.6 (2010): 850-877.*

And juries actually find defendants guilty less often if they're wearing glasses. It's known as the nerd defense. *Source: Brown, Michael J., Ernesto Henriquez, and Jennifer Groscup. "The Effects of Eyeglasses and Race on Juror Decisions Involving a Violent Crime." American Journal of Forensic Psychology 26.2 (2008): 25.*

These biases are so powerful there's actually an entire industry of highly paid trial consultants who help lawyers learn and exploit them. *Source: Benforado, Adam. Unfair. Ch.11.* In some cases, the consultants even screen potential jurors' Facebook pages to decide who to keep and who to send home. *Source: Campoy, Ana and Ashby Jones. Searching for Details Online, Lawyers Facebook the Jury. Wall Street Journal. Dow Jones and Company, 22 Feb. 2011. Web.*

These biases may sound trivial, but the effect they have on cases can be devastating.

ADAM BENFORADO,

Law Professor:

Adam Benforado: "My research is all about the hidden biases in our legal system. For example, political biases can be far more influential on the outcome of a case than what the law actually says. So, in date rape cases, older, more conservative women are far more likely to acquit than younger, more liberal women, regardless of how the law actually defines rape."

So justice is, in fact, not blind.

Adam Benforado: "Our juries all see the world through the tinted lenses of their own biases, which is one of the reasons why black defendants fare so much worse in our system than white defendants. We've all been exposed to damaging stereotypes that link blackness with crime and violence. This can lead juries to assign African American defendants longer sentences than white defendants, because they implicitly see them as more of a threat." *Source: Eberhardt, Jennifer L., et al. "Looking Deathworthy Perceived Stereotypicality of Black Defendants Predicts Capital-Sentencing Outcomes." Psychological Science 17.5 (2006): 383-386.*

And today, is there not a half-billion-dollar industry dedicated to exploiting those biases? *Source: Benforado, Adam. Unfair: The New Science of Criminal Injustice. New York: Crown Publishers, 2015. Web.*

Adam Benforado: "Bingo. Lawyers pay trial consultants huge sums to ensure that they have the most biased juries possible in their favor, which means that a case can be won based on the selection of the jury before the trial even begins."

TO MAKE THINGS WORSE, NOBODY TAKES JURY DUTY SERIOUSLY

Not even the government.

In some states, jury duty pays as little as four dollars an hour. We actually pay the people handing out death sentences less than the people handing out fast food. *Source: Renzulli, Kerri Anne. "How Being a Juror Is Worse Than Working at McDonald's." Money. Time Inc., 19 Feb. 2015. Web.*

Pay is so low, we treat jury duty like it's some sort of punishment. In some cities, the turnout is so bad, they've had to postpone murder trials. *Source: Ferguson, Andrew Guthrie. "A Juror Bill of Rights." The Atlantic. Atlantic Media Company, 11 Sep. 2015. Web.* And even when people do show up, they'll say just about anything to get out of it.

Think about that: Your fate is being decided by a random person who's paid poverty wages, and would rather be doing literally anything else. Is it any wonder they fall back on irrational biases?

EVER WONDER WHY...

Ever wonder exactly why we have a secret service?

Originally the Secret Service had nothing to do with protecting the president, and everything to do with protecting the moolah.

It all started back in the 1800s, when each bank had to design its own money.

The designs were so different, it was incredibly easy to counterfeit money. Over one third of the nation's bills were fake. *Source: Time., April 14, 2015.*

So, on April 14, 1865, Abraham Lincoln created the Secret Service.

Unfortunately, he should have given them two jobs, because John Wilkes Booth assassinated him that exact same day.

Even after Lincoln's assassination, the Secret Service's duties still didn't include protecting the president. It wasn't until after the deaths of Lincoln in 1865, James Garfield in 1881, and William McKinley in 1901, that anyone was like, "hey, maybe you should be protecting this guy." *Source: Washington Post. Oct. 2, 2014.*

PUBLIC DEFENDERS FACE INCREDIBLE STRUGGLES

When someone can't afford counsel, public defenders have to step in. Over 80 percent of people charged with a crime require the help of public defenders. *Source: Mosteller, Robert P. "Failures of the American Adversarial System to Protect the Innocent and Conceptual Advantages in the Inquisitorial Design for Investigative Fairness." North Carolina Journal of International Law & Commercial Regulation 36.2 (2011).*

The fact is, the deck is stacked against public defenders and their clients in every single case. First of all, there just—straight up—aren't enough of public defenders doing this work, because this job means turning down a lucrative career. On average, lawyers at big private firms earn up to double what public defenders make. *Source: "Some Associate Salaries Retreat from Their High But Remain Far Ahead of Salaries for Public Service Attorneys." National Association for Law Placement, 2010.*

Instead, public defenders earn peanuts—and their cases are ridiculous. *Source: Van Brunt, Alexa. "Poor people rely on public defenders who are too overworked to defend them." The Guardian. Guardian Media Group, 17 Jun. 2015. Web.*

Some of public defenders have over 2,000 cases a year.

At that rate, it's impossible to spend enough time on each case. One public defender in Minnesota only had about twelve minutes per client. *Source: Mador, Jessica. "A public defender's day: 12 minutes per client." MPR News. Minnesota Public Radio, 29 Nov. 2010. Web.*

In one case, the public defender had to represent multiple people facing life sentences on the same week they passed the bar exam. *Source: Peng, Tina. "I'm a public defender. It's impossible for me to do a good job representing my clients." Washington Post. Nash Holdings LLC, 3 Sep. 2015. Web.*

PUBLIC DEFENDERS ARE UNDERSTAFFED BECAUSE THEY'RE UNDERFUNDED

In California, for every dollar spent on the prosecution, only fifty-three cents is spent on indigent defense. *Source: Benner, Laurence A. "The Presumption of Guilt: Systemic Factors that Contribute to Ineffective Assistance of Counsel in California." California Western Law Review 45.263 (2009).* In 2007, prosecutors received 3.5 billion dollars more than public defenders. *Source: Waxman, Simon. "Pleading Out: America's Broken Public Defense System." Los Angeles Review of Books, 18 Mar. 2013. Web.*

Yeah, a few more, but not enough to justify the fact that they have five times the staff we do. And think about how hard it is to play defense when it's five against one.

Remember those fancy trial consultants? Public defenders can't afford them. Some demand 300,000 dollars just to work one case.

Public defenders are so underfunded, New Orleans even had to start refusing new cases. *Source: "New Orleans Public Defenders Refuse New Cases To Highlight Underfunding." All Things Considered. National Public Radio, 29 Jan. 2016. Web.*

And, in South Dakota, they actually charge people for public defenders.

Yep, a free lawyer costs you 92 dollars an hour. *Source: Walker, Mark. "In S.D., right to an attorney comes with a price." The Argus Leader. Gannett Company, 8 Mar. 2016. Web.*

The government guaranteed attorneys to people too poor to afford them, then charges clients for those very attorneys.

This problem dwarfs all the other ones.

The government set up a justice system where the prosecution and defense compete to win cases, then systematically provided one side with massive resources, while starving the other. The entire game is rigged.

AS NOT SEEN ON TV

When the writers began pitching narrative ideas for the season, they thought Rhea's character would be a scientist, like Adam's real-life sister. But making her a lawyer instead worked better narratively, and still let the writers tease out a friendly rivalry between the two, which gets resolved on Christmas. After all, how could anyone keep feuding with a sibling who has such a similar hairdo?

BUT IT'S POSSIBLE
TO CHANGE IT

The justice system isn't perfect, that's because it's made up of people—and people aren't perfect either. But we have to trust that there are people working every single to day to make it better.

And you can make a difference too—with jury duty.

Every few years, every American is given the chance to take part in the system. For that one case, you have the power to fix these problems. All you have to do is show up, check your biases, and make sure you hear both sides of the case.

ADAM RUINS
CHRISTMAS

DIRECTOR: TIM WILKIME

ORIGINAL AIR DATE: DECEMBER 20, 2016

Ho, ho...uh oh. Turns out the real story behind Jolly Old St. Nick is actually pretty creepy, modern Santa was created by commercialism only a century ago, and gift-giving actually hurts the economy. Now, where are the milk and cookies?

CHRIST DIDN'T USE TO BE A PART OF CHRISTMAS

Historically, Christmas was actually a really raucous holiday. And most of our Christmas traditions have really un-Christian origins.

The real story of the holiday season starts over 2,000 years ago during the Roman Empire. In December, Romans celebrated a holiday called Saturnalia to mark the end of the harvest. It was a wild party involving gambling, singing, and even cross-dressing. *Source: "Did the Romans Invent Christmas?" BBC Religion and Ethics. British Broadcasting Corporation, 17 Dec. 2012. Web.*

And in Northern Europe, a drunken festival called "Yule" celebrated the birth of the sun. Families would burn the biggest log they could find and celebrate around evergreen trees to ward off winter depression. *Source: Purdue, A.W. "Tracing the Festive Light Fantastic: Resources." Times Educational Supplement. TES Global, 14 Dec. 2012. Web.*

THAT DECEMBER 25 THING

No one really knows for certain when Jesus was born. But we do know that when Christianity took hold of Europe in the fifth century, some common folk refused to part with these pagan parties. So, Christian leaders gradually transformed these popular traditions into a celebration of Jesus' birth.

Inserting Christ into these winter festivals was basically a civic compromise. Make the party about Jesus and you can keep getting jiggy with it. *Source: Bowler, Gerry. Christmas in the Crosshairs: Two Thousand Years of Denouncing and Defending the World's Most Celebrated Holiday. New York: Oxford University Press, 2017. Print.*

But it didn't change much.

Christmas stayed a debauched, violent booze-fest for a long time. For over a thousand years, Christmas was more like a terrifying Mardi Gras. In England, drunken mobs would take over the streets, and a beggar would be crowned the Lord of Missed Rule.

The mobs would bang on rich people's doors and demand to be served the best food and drink they had. And if they refused, they were threatened with Christmas violence. *Source: Strutt, Joseph. The Sports and Pastimes of the People of England. London: Methuen & Co., 1801. Web.*

When Puritans came to America, they decided Christmas had no place in a Christian nation and banned it.

In some communities, if you exhibited Christmas spirit, you were even forced to pay a fine. *Source: Woolf, Christopher. "America's First 'War on Christmas.'" PRI's The World. Public Radio International, Dec. 23, 2015. Web.*

Thanks to the legacy of these rules, Christmas ended up pretty unpopular in America. But all that changed in the nineteenth century. As immigrants flooded into America, they brought with them a love of Christmas and their own traditions. These seeped into the popular culture, and a new American Christmas began to take hold. *Source: Voice of America. Dec. 21, 2014.*

And now, we treat Christmas like it's always been a sacred Christian celebration. But the historical truth is, these winter festivities have pagan roots, with drunken traditions that a lot of Christians straight up hated for like, a thousand years.

Celebrating Christmas as the birth of Jesus is a wonderful tradition. But it's just as historically accurate to get drunk in the woods, or bang on a rich person's door and threaten them with violence. So instead of worrying that Christmas isn't Christian anymore, why don't we just let people celebrate the way they want?

Ever wonder why *It's a Wonderful Life* plays on TV every year during Christmastime?

Now it's a holiday classic. But it didn't used to be. When *It's a Wonderful Life* came out in 1946, it was a massive flop. So much so, that when the copyright came up for renewal in the '70s, no one even bothered to extend it.

When the copyright lapsed, the movie fell into the public domain, and it became free to air on television. So, cheapskate TV stations started airing it nonstop during Christmas. *Source: Slate. Dec 21, 1999.*

And thus, *It's a Wonderful Life* was cemented into the imagination of a generation.

Thanks to the public domain, we have this beloved Christmas classic. And every time you watch it, a cable host gets his wings.

GIVING GIFTS IS BAD FOR THE ECONOMY

Gift giving may feel nice, but it makes no economic sense. In fact, it actually destroys up to 20 billion dollars in value every year.

First, let's define "economic value."

The value of an object is the maximum amount that its owner would be willing to pay for it. Or simply put, how much it's worth to you. Add all these amounts together and that's the total value of everything you've bought.

And, if you value something at, say one-hundred dollars, but you only paid fifty dollars, then you literally created fifty dollars in value.

JOEL WALDFOGEL,

Economist, Carlson School of Management
University of Minnesota:

Joel Waldfogel: "When we buy gifts, we do so with the best of intentions. But while we're really good at knowing what we like, we're pretty terrible at guessing what other people would value."

If you get someone a shirt and paid fifty dollars for it, but they're only gonna wear it to bed and value it at maybe fifteen dollars, then congrats. You just destroyed thirty-five dollars of value.

Joel Waldfogel: "Now sometimes, we get it right and buy the perfect gift. But on average, gifts are worth 18 percent less per dollar spent to their recipients than things we buy for ourselves." *Source: Waldfogel, Joel. Scroogenomics: Why You Shouldn't Buy Presents for the Holidays. Princeton: Princeton University Press, 2009.*

And statistically, spouses are actually the best gift givers. You know who's worse? Parents. And according to Joel's research, there's not much worse than the dreaded aunt. *Source: Waldfogel, Joel. Scroogenomics: Why You Shouldn't Buy Presents for the Holidays. Princeton: Princeton University Press, 2009.*

Joel Waldfogel: "And when you add up the waste across all the gifts in the economy, we're destroying more than twenty billion dollars per year."

That doesn't mean we need to stop giving gifts...but we need to be a whole lot smarter about it.

Joel Waldfogel: "We should just be extra careful in those situations where we're giving to people whose preference we don't know."

We can make more use of tools like online wish lists and gift cards that enable the recipient to pick the gift that they want. That way, we can all have a more economically efficient holiday.

EVER WONDER WHY...

Ever wonder why no two snowflakes are alike? Well, you shouldn't, because that ain't strictly true. Back in 1988, cloud scientist Nancy Knight did some research high above Wisconsin. *Source: The Sun-Sentinel. Aug. 4. 1988.*

She studied a bunch of high altitude snow crystals and found two snowflakes that looked completely identical.

Turns out, snowflakes in their earliest stages are simple six-sided prisms and these boring flakes can look really similar. But as they fall, they travel through different atmospheres. And that's when the snowflakes really become different. *Source: Australian Broadcasting Corporation. Nov. 13, 2006.*

Depending on temperature and humidity, a snowflake can drastically change its shape and style. By the time the snowflake reaches the ground, it looks nothing like it did in the clouds.

So while you may never spot two identical snowflakes down here on the ground, up there in the clouds, snowflakes aren't really that special at all.

THE TRUE HISTORY OF SANTA CLAUS IS... KINDA CREEPY

No, Santa wasn't invented by Coca Cola. But! In the early twentieth century, Coca Cola was going through a series of PR scandals— including the fact that their cola was made with cocaine. *Source: Pendergrast, Mark. For God, Country and Coca-Cola: the Unauthorized History of the Great American Soft Drink and the Company That Makes It. New York: Scribner's, 1993. Web.*

To appear more loveable, Coca Cola advertised using a rosy-cheeked, red-suited, family-friendly St. Nick. But they didn't invent him. They just used his image to make a buck.

Santa has been used for weird campaigns throughout history. In olden days, he was often portrayed as a boozer. But the temperance movement made him sober to promote prohibition.

One version of Santa was used in twentieth-century socialist campaigns.

While in 1874 Mississippi, there was actually a Santa-themed KKK rally. *Source: Bowler, Gerry. Santa Claus, A Biography. Toronto: McClelland & Stewart, 2007.*

And yet, somehow, early Santas were way weirder.

Before 1880, Santa didn't even live at the North Pole. That idea was invented by Thomas Nast, who drew Santa recording kids' behavior from a giant telescope. *Source: Kennedy, Robert C. "On this Day: Santa Claus and His Works." Learning Center, New York Times. The New York Times Company, 25 Dec. 2001. Web.*

And the European precursors to Santa were even more messed up.

Germanic nations replaced St. Nick with baby Jesus and a demon named Krampus, who dragged bad kids to hell. *Source: Handwerk, Brian. "St. Nicholas to Santa: The Surprising Origins of Mr. Claus." National Geographic. National Geographic Society, Dec. 20, 2013. Web.*

The Dutch believed St. Nicholas himself brought the presents. But instead of an elf, he was accompanied by a literal slave named Black Peter, often portrayed by a white person in black face. *Source: Noel, Melissa. "The Fight Against 'Black Pete', a Holiday Blackface Tradition." NBC News. NBC Universal, 23 Dec. 2015. Web.*

St. Nick *was* real, though.

St. Nicholas of Myra was the patron saint of gift-giving and children.

But, yeah, he was creepy.

Jolly Old St. Nick loved giving gifts, especially to young girls. He would sneak into their houses in the middle of the night and leave gold in their stockings so they wouldn't become prostitutes. *Source: Handwerk, Brian. "St. Nicholas to Santa: The Surprising Origins of Mr. Claus." National Geographic. National Geographic Society, Dec. 20, 2013. Web.*

And the reason he's the patron saint of children is even stranger.

According to legend, St. Nick found a pickle barrel. But it wasn't just any pickle barrel. It was full of dead and dismembered children. And St. Nick, with the power of a holy miracle, brought all those chunks of dead children back to life.

AS NOT SEEN ON TV ✂

This was a really difficult episode to research, because so much of the information comes from pagan folklore, and wasn't necessarily written down at the time. There's also so much misinformation, since popular outlets run Christmas content that isn't necessarily held to rigorous academic standards. It can be really tough to suss out the scholarly from the sensational!

JUST CELEBRATE HOW YOU WANT!

All traditions started somewhere and all traditions have changed.

The true meaning of Christmas is whatever you want it to be. Because it's all made up.

You can make your own traditions.

EPISODE TWENTY-SIX

ADAM RUINS
GOING GREEN

DIRECTOR: TIM WILKIME
ORIGINAL AIR DATE: DECEMBER 27, 2016

Going green ain't quite as great as it's made out to be. The famous "Crying Indian" PSA wasn't quite what we thought, there's a surprising history behind the concept of "litterbugs," and electric cars and green products don't make the positive impact they're supposed to.

ALL IT TAKES TO SAVE THE ENVIRONMENT IS FOR EACH OF US TO DO OUR PART!

That kind of thinking is gonna lead us to a trashtastrophe.

Using green products, picking up your own litter, and making small sacrifices in your life, will not stop climate change. Those things will never be enough. And that personal responsibility you feel is just the result of an old ad campaign.

And everything about it is wrong.

First of all, the Indian in the ad, Iron Eyes Cody, was actually an Italian man named Espera de Corti. *Source: Ryder, Katie. "Hollywood Indian." Paris Review. The Paris Review Foundation, 1 Aug. 2013. Web.* This guy lied for his entire life about his heritage and was basically the Native American Rachel Dolezal.

And that's not even the worst part. The filthy truth is, this message was designed by the can and bottle industry to shift the blame from them—to you.

For decades, we had an effective system for reducing litter. After people finished their soda, they returned the bottles, and the manufacturers would wash and reuse them. *Source: Jorgensen, Finn Arne. "A Pocket History of Bottle Recycling." The Atlantic. Atlantic Media Company, 27 Feb. 2013. Web.*

But in the '50s, a group of greedy companies switched to disposable cans and bottles to cut costs.

After they went disposable, we started going through twice as many bottles and cans.

Source: Rogers, Heather. Gone Tomorrow: The Hidden Life of Garbage. New York: New Press, 2005.

The switch caused so much outrage that in 1953, Vermont introduced a law that actually banned disposable bottles. *Source: Rogers, Heather. Gone Tomorrow: The Hidden Life of Garbage. New York: New Press, 2005.*

Bottles were filling up their farms, and their big beautiful cows were eating them and dying. *Source: Fenton, John H. "VERMONT'S SESSION HAS*

BUDGET CLASH; Taxes Urged in Place of Plan by Gov. Emerson to Balance Costs by Using Surplus." New York Times. New York Times Company, 1 Feb. 1953. Web.

Their business model threatened, the container industry whipped up a plan and coined the term "litterbug." *Source: Plumer, Bradford. "The Origins of Anti-Litter Campaigns." Mother Jones. Foundation for National Progress, 22 May 2006. Web.*

With the help of over twenty companies, they founded the original anti-litter group, Keep America Beautiful.

These companies actually popularized the term litterbug, and shifted the litter blame from themselves to you. And all of this culminated in Keep America Beautiful's most famous ad: "The Crying Indian." *Source: "Pollution: Keep America Beautiful—Iron Eyes Cody." Ad Council, 2016. Web.*

The most famous PSA in history was actually a piece of corporate propaganda.

And all of this totally worked. Bottle bans were struck down, and Americans started blaming ourselves for the litter problem.

Now we're stuck with disposables. And every year, over one hundred billion beverage containers end up wasted—either in landfills, incinerators or, yeah, just plain littered. *Source: "Bottled Up (2000-2010) – Beverage Container Recycling Stagnates." Container Recycling Institute, 2010. Web.*

To be clear: If you litter, you're a jerk. But these companies threw out an effective recycling system and instead asked us to pick up their trash. And their marketing campaign helped create an entire green culture that blames individuals for pollution, rather than the companies making it.

DON'T DITCH YOUR HYBRID FOR A NEW ELECTRIC

You should wait.

If you're selling that perfectly good car to buy a brand new Tesla, you're not doing a good deed. You're just buying a bright, shiny, potentially ecologically problematic toy.

Sure, electric cars like the Tesla are the sexy new thing.

And a big part of their appeal is that car companies have marketed them as greener than a pocket square on St. Paddy's day.

Turns out that message is pretty sketchy. Look, electric cars are more energy efficient than gas cars, but where do you think that energy comes from?

It comes from the energy grid.

If you buy an electric car today, you're just shifting your fuel source from the gas pump to a power plant. And if those power plants burn coal, driving an electric car might actually put more CO2 into the air than a hybrid.

Source: Oremus, Will. "How Green Is a

AS NOT SEEN ON TV ✂

Practically every segment of the show gets some feedback, both positive and negative. But more viewers than usual took issue with Act II of this episode, on electric cars. The show later responded to the criticisms in a Medium post, which was a new way of continuing the dialog after the episode airs. That's one reason Adam is so committed to showing sources on-screen, and putting bibliographies online—no question is settled, and new information and contexts can change things! That's what Adam does when he "ruins" things: he puts ideas in a new light, and asks people to look at things in new ways. Viewers can do that, too!

Tesla, Really?" Slate. Graham Holdings Company, 9 Sep. 2013. Web. According to one study, even if a third of all drivers switch to electric cars, the carbon savings could be negligible. *Source: Babaee, Samaneh, Ajay S. Nagpure, and Joseph F. DeCarolis. "How much do electric drive vehicles matter to future US emissions?" Environmental science & technology 48.3 (2014): 1382-1390.*

And the dream of our energy all coming from solar, wind, and water, is a long way off. In fact, your new Tesla will probably break down before that happens. And in the meantime, you're gonna be pumping out a ton of CO2 from everything that goes into just making the car. *Source: Berners-Lee, Mike, and Duncan Clark. "What's the carbon footprint of...a new car?" The Guardian. Guardian Media Group, 23 Sep. 2010. Web.*

Building an electric car requires steel, copper, and aluminum, just like a regular car. But worse, their batteries are made of rare metals that take intensive mining. *Source: Wade, Lizzie. "Tesla's Electric Cars Aren't As Green As You Might Think." Wired. Conde Nast, 31 Mar. 2016. Web.*

And even the mere act of putting the car together produces greenhouse gases. Add that up, and if we all ditched our trusty old cars in favor of brand new electrics, we'd actually end up increasing our carbon footprint. *Source: Berners-Lee, Mike, and Duncan Clark. "What's the carbon footprint of...a new car?" The Guardian. Guardian Media Group, 23 Sep. 2010. Web.*

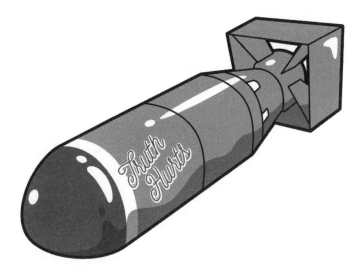

MIKE BERNERS-LEE,

Carbon Emissions Expert:

"While electric cars are more efficient, manufacturing typically adds about 50 percent to the total carbon footprint. So, if you buy a new car too often, you could completely undo all the carbon savings that you might get from buying an electric car. If you really want to help save the environment, the best thing you can do is to reduce the amount you drive, and to drive your current car as long as possible, provided it's reasonably efficient. But if your car is beyond repair and you absolutely need to buy a new one, then go ahead, buy yourself a nice, small electric car. Perhaps even a used one."

When it comes to saving the planet, the efficiency of your car's engine is small potatoes. The real problem is that Americans bought 17.5 million cars last year and drove a total of 2.7 trillion miles. *Source: U.S. Department of Transportation, Federal Highway Administration. Annual Vehicle Distance Traveled in Miles and Related Data - 2014 by Highway Category and Vehicle Type. 2015. Web.* Buying another car just isn't gonna fix that.

And if you're not careful, these companies will use that desire to help the planet to sell you more stuff that's hurting the planet. Buying green products won't solve the problem because buying stuff is part of the problem. We need to reduce what we buy and reuse what we have. We can't shop our way out of this.

REDUCING YOUR CARBON FOOTPRINT IS WAY HARDER THAN PEOPLE THINK

And, if you wanna ditch vehicles to walk instead, know this: Walking isn't always the greenest thing you can do.

In fact, our carbon system is so complex that a lot of what we think will reduce our carbon footprints actually makes things worse.

Let's say you and your kid go to a fast food place. You each ate a burger and went for a walk. So the burger fueled your walk. But that burger came from a cow. And the cow got most of its fuel from grain and cows need a lot of grain to survive.

And producing all that grain takes a ton of energy, which often comes from coal, gas, and oil, a.k.a., fossil fuels. You have to burn fifty-four calories of fossil fuel just to make one calorie of beef protein. *Source: U.S. could feed 800 million people with grain that livestock eat, Cornell ecologist advises animal scientists. Cornell Chronicle. Cornell University, 7 Aug. 1997. Web.*

And because we have so many cows and farms, agriculture accounts for up to one-third of all greenhouse gas emissions. Add all that together, and this fuel can actually have a larger carbon footprint than this fuel. So if your walk to work is powered by burgers, you're not a hybrid, you're a gas guzzler. *Source: Berners-Lee, Mike. How Bad Are Bananas? The Carbon Footprint of Everything. Vancouver: Greystone Books, 2011. Web.*

BEING A VEGETARIAN DOESN'T NECESSARILY HELP

Maybe that walk we mentioned was powered by asparagus, not burgers.

Great.

Except asparagus can actually be one of the most wasteful foods.

Veggies like asparagus were likely flown a long distance to get here. And air freighting produce is one-hundred-times worse for the environment than shipping by boat. *Source: Charles, Dan. "Top 5 Ways Asparagus, A Rite Of Spring, Can Still Surprise." All Things Considered. National Public Radio, 13 Mar. 2014. Web.*

And when they're out of season, the same is likely true of baby corn, baby carrots, snap peas, small green beans, okra, shelled peas, lettuce, blueberries, raspberries, and strawberries. *Source: Berners-Lee, Mike. How Bad Are Bananas? The Carbon Footprint of Everything. Vancouver: Greystone Books, 2011. Web.* The truth is, when you grab a vegetable, it can be almost impossible to tell how big its carbon footprint really is. Even in a fancy organic store, the produce aisle is full of carbon landmines.

EVEN BANANAS AREN'T PERFECT

They're still part of the same system that's destroying our planet. If you really want to calculate your carbon footprint, you have to look at the whole picture.

Think about the banana companies' corporate offices, which create their own emissions. Like the coffee they supply to their employees. Coffee that required water and energy to grow and ship. And that shipping company provided uniforms for their drivers, uniforms that required zippers. Zippers made out of metals which needed to be mined from the Earth. And during lunch at the zipper mine, what did they serve? Bananas.

We live in an infinite web of carbon pollution. The number of variables at play is so vast, they're impossible for a single person to even calculate—let alone reduce.

BUT WE'RE TRYING OUR BEST!

And that is commendable. But the fact is, this problem is way too big for our individual consumer choices to solve. Our entire way of life is the problem.

Some time ago, humanity discovered vast deposits of fuel buried deep within the Earth. We learned to extract it, burn it for energy, and release it into the air. And about 150 years ago, we rebuilt our entire civilization around that energy source.

We burn it to travel. We burn it to eat. We burn it to live. Fossil fuels brought about one of the greatest increases in standard of living in human history. We could never go back.

But by burning this incredible fuel source, we are also inexorably heating the Earth. 2015 was the hottest year since we started keeping records in 1880. And thanks to rising ocean temperatures, average sea levels have already risen about eight inches. *Source: National Aeronautics and Space Administration. Global Land-Ocean Temperature Index. 2015. Web.*

DR. DALE JAMIESON, PHD,

Professor of Environmental Studies, NYU:

Dr. Dale Jamieson: "We've already done so much damage to the atmosphere that we'll be lucky if we can hold the warming to two degrees Celsius. Just two degrees of warming could cause huge droughts, massive wildfires, the loss of many species, the collapse of our agricultural productivity. And the rising sea levels could make our coastal cities uninhabitable."

And remember, two degrees of warming is the best we can realistically hope for. The question isn't, will warming happen? The question is, how bad will it be?

Dr. Dale Jamieson: "The sad truth is that we've already put so much carbon dioxide in the atmosphere, that we're more than halfway towards that two degrees centigrade limit."

And right now, companies and countries already own enough fossil fuel in reserves to meet that limit five times over. *Source: McKibben, Bill. "Global Warming's Terrifying New Math." Rolling Stone. Wenner Media LLC, 19 Jul. 2012. Web.*

To keep those fossil fuels in the ground, those companies and countries would have to give up trillions of dollars...and we'd have to change our entire way of life.

And if we burn it, it won't be our planet anymore.

THERE'S STILL HOPE

But you can't do it by yourself.

We have to do it together. Buying greener stuff and walking to work is great, but it's not enough. The entire world has to come together to solve this problem.

And that's what's happening.

In 2015, nearly every country in the world met as one and for the first time, signed a treaty to curb carbon emissions. It was called the Paris Agreement. *Source: "'Today is an historic day,' says Ban, as 175 countries sign Paris climate accord." UN News Centre. United Nations, 22 Apr. 2016. Web.*

Dr. Dale Jamieson: "Each country agreed to be accountable for reducing its emissions every five years. That's a big deal. It proves that international cooperation on climate change is possible."

The Paris Agreement is just a first step. Its emissions limits are non-binding and by itself, it won't stop us from exceeding two degrees of warming. *Source: Cassidy, John. "A Skeptical Note on the Paris Climate Deal." New Yorker. Conde Nast, 14 Dec. 2015. Web.*

No matter how tough things are now, we can always make things better for the kids that come later. And the Paris Agreement is a big step on that road.

In addition to reducing, re-using, and all those good things, you have to take individual action to encourage collective responsibility. You can tell your politicians to uphold the Paris Agreement, which some localities are—despite President Donald Trump backing the U.S. out—and build on its success. And, you can raise your voice and encourage others to do the same.

Humans have changed the Earth in profound ways, and we're gonna keep changing it. But it's up to us what kind of earth we're making.

We need to leave a better world for those who come after us.